THE
SOLO TRAVEL
HANDBOOK

Practical tips and inspiration for a safe, fun and fearless trip

CONTENTS

BEFORE YOU GO

ON THE ROAD

DECIDING TO GO

INSPIRATION: 10 GREAT TRIPS FOR SOLO TRAVELLERS

INSPIRATION: SOLO TRAVEL TALES

Budget breakdown

$ = BUDGET
$$ = MID-RANGE
$$$ = TOP-END

LGBT-friendliness indicator

LONELY PLANET WRITERS HAVE RATED DESTINATIONS FROM 1 TO 5 BASED ON THEIR FRIENDLINESS TOWARDS SAME-SEX COUPLES. 1 INDICATES THE LEAST LGBT-FRIENDLY PLACES, AND 5 REPRESENTS THE DESTINATIONS THAT ARE MOST WELCOMING.

DECIDING TO GO

WHY GO SOLO?

Powder-white sand beaches. Lush, tropical rainforests. Vibrant, ancient cultures. Local markets that almost literally pop with colour. Not a day goes by where you don't secretly wish you were living your Instagram feed, but you can't convince anyone to take a trip with you. So, why don't you go by yourself?

Sure, the idea of travelling alone might sound daunting to a first-timer. Too much, even. But with a little bit of confidence and a generous dose of preparation, you'll find that travelling solo won't just be fun, but more rewarding than you ever imagined.

THE PRACTICAL PERKS

Solo travel is the ultimate indulgence, because it's all about you. When you're in charge of your own schedule, you can go where you want and do what you want, when you want and how you want. You're free to meet new people – which tends to be easier when you're travelling solo – and really soak up the destination without any distractions. You can travel as fast as you want, or take as much downtime as you like, without having to justify your choices to anyone but yourself. Enjoy it!

THE PERSONAL JOURNEY

Solo travel offers the ultimate opportunity for self-reflection and development. At home, our friends, families, employers and colleagues all play roles in influencing the way we live our lives. Travelling alone, you can escape these influences and make your own decisions. Without a travel partner to delegate some of those decisions to, your problem-solving ability increases, making you a more independent, more fearless solo traveller in the process. Expect to get to know yourself better, discovering strengths you didn't know you had, as well as identifying weaknesses you may wish to work on. Embrace it.

CHALLENGING THE SINGLE STIGMA

There must be something wrong with you if you travel alone, said no one ever. Yet, somehow, a stigma still persists. Fortunately, it's changing. A raft of recent studies have shown solo travel is on the increase and, as more people begin to embrace it, the image of solo travel is being redefined as a luxury rather than some sort of back-up plan. If you're living a fabulously independent life at home, there's no reason why you can't have a similarly fantastic experience on the road. Own it.

SO, WHAT ARE YOU WAITING FOR? TURN THE PAGE, GET INSPIRED AND GET READY TO REALISE YOUR TRAVEL DREAMS – ALL BY YOURSELF.

WHAT'S STOPPING YOU?

You can make a million excuses for not wanting to travel on your own, and you'll always find more – unless you make the conscious choice to confront your solo-travel fears. To give you a friendly push in the right direction, we've broken down some of the most common solo-travel fears, so they don't seem so scary at all.

© PERFECT LAZYBONES / SHUTTERSTOCK

'I DON'T THINK I'M BRAVE OR OUTGOING ENOUGH'

Travelling solo isn't necessarily synonymous with being an adrenalin junkie or even an extrovert. If you're the shy or timid type, ease into solo travel by taking a tour so you can get used to new destinations before breaking away to do your own thing, or choose an easy travel destination – perhaps in your home country – where you can work on building your confidence in more familiar surroundings. Being somewhat forced to talk to people while travelling alone, whether it's to ask for directions or order a meal, has a wonderful way of bringing people out of their shells.

'I'M WORRIED ABOUT THE COST'

There is no rule that says solo travel is more expensive than group travel. It can often be cheaper, as you don't have to compromise on where you stay, eat or play. Opt for tour companies that don't charge a single supplement and/or match you with a roommate (p27). Consider staying in a dorm to cut down on hotel-room costs, ask about discounts for single occupancy.

'IS IT EVEN SAFE?'

This is a perfectly legitimate concern for every traveller, and one that should be kept in mind with regard to all decisions you make on the road. While travelling alone is often seen as riskier than travelling in a group, this is not always the case. Travelling solo, you are forced to be aware of your personal safety, whereas in a group you may let your guard down and expose your vulnerability. Choosing a destination where you feel comfortable travelling is the first step to keeping this fear in check. See p86 for more tips on staying safe on the road as a solo traveller.

'i FEEL GUiLTY ABOUT LEAVING MY LOVED ONES BEHIND'

The people who love you should not make you feel guilty for wanting to follow your travel dream. Just as they have a responsibility to support you, you also have a responsibility to support them by making an effort to stay in touch and keep them involved in your life while you're on the road. Fortunately, there are now more gadgets and apps than ever to help you stay connected; see p79 for the lowdown.

'TAKING MY FIRST SOLO TRiP WAS THE BEST THiNG i'VE EVER DONE FOR MY RELATiONSHiP'

'I was in a relationship when I took my first solo trip and I felt incredibly selfish about travelling at a time when my boyfriend couldn't. I booked my one-way flight on an impulse and, when I told him, he assured me it would be OK because he'd travelled solo himself and understood my need to have this experience. Prioritising my needs during the trip sparked my love for travel. Today, we're happily married and we run a travel blog together full-time.' – Phoebe Lee, travel blogger, littlegreybox.net. Read about Phoebe's first solo trip on p144.

'i'M SCARED i'LL BE LONELY OR GET HOMESiCK'

There are times while travelling alone that you will be forced to make do with your own company. Enjoy it. Take the opportunity to observe and savour the world around you, read a book or start a diary. Most solo travellers will find that it is actually easier to meet people when they are on their own, with locals, hotel staff and waiters often going out of their way to engage solo travellers in conversation. There are also plenty of great ways to meet people on the road, even in places you'd least expect; see p66 for Lonely Planet's top 10.

'QUITTING MY HIGH-POWERED JOB TO TRAVEL WAS EXACTLY WHAT MY CAREER NEEDED'

'After spending 15 years building a successful career in fashion, people thought I was crazy when I gave it all up to walk solo across Spain. But it was a case of now or never. I'd always wanted to start my own business but had never been brave enough to do it. I figured if I could make this walk by myself, I could do anything. And that's what happened. After walking 775km, I found the strength to believe in my idea and back myself, and I've never looked back.' – *Kat Fahey, wedding planner.* Read about Kat's life-changing solo trip on p152.

'WHAT ABOUT MY CAREER?'

Whether you're quitting your job to travel, or taking a 10-day break that feels more like a year in your fast-paced life, focus on the positives. You may miss out on a company event or an opportunity for a promotion, but you'll gain skills on the road that may very well land you the role of your dreams down the track. At the very least, a bit of time out can help you to reassess what you really want out of your career, so you can return with guns blazing. For advice on working on the road, flick to p69.

'AM I TOO OLD TO TRAVEL SOLO?'

Just because you didn't take a gap year after school or university doesn't mean you have (literally) missed the boat. Whether you're 26 or 56, there are destinations, tour companies and travel communities that cater to solo travellers just like you; a little bit of research will help you find your tribe. Even if you do end up on a tour bus with people 20 years older or younger than you, use it as an opportunity to learn a bit more about a different generation.

SO, WHAT ARE YOU WAITING FOR? THERE'S A WHOLE WORLD OUT THERE. PUSH YOUR FEARS ASIDE AND JUST GO!

10 THINGS YOU LEARN ABOUT YOURSELF WHILE TRAVELLING SOLO

If you travel alone, you may learn just as much about yourself as the destinations you visit. These lessons can then be transferred to all areas of your life.

1 YOU LEARN WHAT KIND OF TRAVELLER YOU ARE

When you don't have to fit in with anyone else's travel preferences, your personal travel style becomes clear. Perhaps you realise you prefer exploring at a fast pace, or otherwise enjoy having more time to smell the roses. Maybe you discover your inner party animal, or you find that you like getting up early to sightsee before the crowds arrive. This intel will help you better plan future solo trips.

2 YOU LEARN TO BE MORE OPEN-MINDED

When you travel alone, your assumptions and beliefs are tested more than ever. With no one by your side to back up your prejudices, you'll learn to open your mind to new ways of living, and re-evaluate any pre-conceived notions about these cultures or customs you may have been harbouring.

© SERGIO BALLIVIAN / 500PX

3 YOU LEARN WHAT YOUR LIMITS ARE

Thought you'd be comfortable enough sleeping in a 20-bed dorm? Figured you'd be tough enough to manage a multi-day wilderness hike without access to a shower? Travelling solo, you'll quickly find out what your limits are, and how comfortable you are pushing them.

4 YOU LEARN TO BE COMFORTABLE BEING ALONE

There might be times when you wish you had someone to share a meal with, but after travelling solo for a while, you learn to be at peace with your own company. After being in a group environment for a few days, you may even find yourself pining for a bit of solitude afterwards.

5 YOU LEARN TO TAKE RESPONSIBILITY

You'll lose bank cards, miss buses, underestimate the amount of time it takes to get to the airport, and forget to book a hostel during a festival period. When travelling solo, you have no one else to blame for your mistakes but yourself. You learn to take full responsibility for them, take the lessons on board, and move on.

6 YOU LEARN TO TRUST YOUR INTUITION

Without a trusted travel partner to help point you in the right (or wrong) direction on the road, you find the courage to trust your own instincts. You have no other choice, after all.

© TOUCHING LIGHT, MOVING YOUR HEART / GETTY IMAGES

7 YOU LEARN WHAT IS IMPORTANT TO YOU IN LIFE

As you are introduced to new people, sights, smells and sounds, you develop the ability to look at your 'real' life at home more objectively. You question whether the habits, goals and lifestyle choices you once thought were important really matter to you as much as you thought they did.

8 YOU LEARN TO LIVE WITH LESS

After travelling for a while, you get used to living with just the essentials. Suddenly the idea of ordering next season's must-have jeans when you have a perfectly good pair at home, or spending an hour on your beauty regime each day that you could be spending at the beach, starts to seem a lot sillier than it once did.

© AHMED KHALIL / 500PX

9 YOU LEARN WHO YOUR REAL FRIENDS ARE

Your true friends and family love you for you, and understand (or at least learn to accept) your need to travel alone. When you return, you'll pick up exactly where you left off. Other people you may have thought you were close to, however, may not relate to the 'new you', and don't have time for the travel stories you've been dying to share with them. Likewise, you may realise that you don't have as much in common with these 'friends' as you thought, and start to re-evaluate the role they play in your life.

10 YOU LEARN THERE IS ALWAYS ROOM IN YOUR LIFE FOR MORE FRIENDS

You'll soon learn that it's easy to make friends travelling solo, with many of the friends you meet on the road ending up being friends for life. Be receptive to other travellers who strike up conversation, taking the time to find out more about what brought them to the very same place you're visiting – you may very well have something in common.

BEFORE YOU GO

PLANNING YOUR ITINERARY

Congratulations! You've cleared the biggest hurdle – making the decision to go – and you're ready to start planning. Every traveller has a different planning style, from winging it to planning every minute. Solo travel offers the flexibility to change your itinerary on a whim, but first-timers would be wise to do a little forward planning to ensure a less stressful trip.

WHAT DO YOU WANT OUT OF YOUR TRIP?

Before deciding where to go, it's important to look at what you want out of your trip, as this could play a significant role in your destination choice. Ask yourself: is this trip to relax or to explore? For self-reflection or self-development? Do I want alone time, or to be surrounded by people? Do I want to learn a new skill? Perhaps it's a combination of reasons.

© SWISSMEDIAVISION / GETTY IMAGES

CHOOSiNG YOUR DESTiNATiON

Cost tends to be a key determining factor in choosing a travel destination. Countries can be roughly classed in three cost tiers. Australia, Canada, Japan, New Zealand, the UK, the US and most of Western Europe (especially Scandinavia) sit in the top tier. The next tier down includes many countries on continental Africa, China, Eastern Europe, South Korea, Russia, Singapore, and the lower countries in South America (Argentina, Brazil, Chile, Uruguay). These places often have one or two cheap aspects, such as food or in some cases lodging, but other costs can be high. The cheapest destination tier includes the rest of the developing world. Most of Southeast Asia, the Indian subcontinent, most of Central America, and the rest of South America are generally much friendlier on a backpacker budget, and the cost of just about everything – food, accommodation and transportation – is lower than in any Western country. That said, if you're only travelling on a short trip, it may be more economical to travel to a more expensive country or city geographically closer to you than heading to a cheaper destination further away.

On top of cost, the other big considerations are your confidence and safety. Do you feel comfortable with the challenge of travelling to a country where you don't speak the language? Will you be on edge all the time if you choose to travel to a region with higher safety risks than you are used to at home? If your answer if yes, but you still want to visit the destination, perhaps a group tour (p117) is the best option for you.

© DAVE AND LES JACOBS / GETTY IMAGES

TiMiNG iT RiGHT

If travel isn't dictated by money, it is dictated by time. There are several factors to consider when it comes to timing your trip right. Firstly, it's important to ensure your chosen destinations are feasible to visit during your travel window. Trying to squeeze four European countries into a single week may leave you feeling like you never properly experienced any of them, while allocating two weeks in Paris may leave you feeling restless after a week.

It's also important to consider the ideal time to travel to your chosen destination – travelling to the Philippines during typhoon season may not bode well for a diving or hiking holiday, while visiting a Muslim country during Ramadan might make it difficult for you to find food during the day. Perhaps the region you wish to visit is politically unstable, and your insurer won't cover you if you decide to travel there at a certain time – or perhaps you suffer from hay fever and your intended destination will be in the middle of flowering season.

© FRANCISCO GONCALVES / GETTY IMAGES

 TOP TIP

'When drawing up a travel itinerary, always check whether any major events are taking place during your intended stay. This can include everything from music festivals and sporting events to public holiday celebrations, all of which can significantly bump up the costs of both flights and accommodation due to high demand. Travelling at peak times, such as local school holidays, is likely to have a similar effect. If you're not travelling to attend an event or because you're a teacher on school break, your wallet will thank you for altering your dates!' *STEPHANIE PARKER, TRAVEL BLOGGER, BIGWORLDSMALLPOCKETS.COM*

Solo Journey Planning Timeline: The Big Trip

☐ ONE YEAR BEFORE

Dream. Think about where you've always wanted to travel, and get inspired by guidebooks, magazines, websites and solo travel blogs.

☐ NINE MONTHS BEFORE

You'll likely have a pretty good idea of how much money you're going to have to work with, and you can compare your budget (p24) against that dream list of destinations you feel comfortable travelling to on your own.

☐ SIX MONTHS BEFORE

Consider whether you will join a group tour, and factor tour options and availability into the travel dates you choose after calibrating for personal commitments and taking into account the optimal time – as you deem it – for visiting your destinations of choice.

LEFT Holi Festival is
a riot of colour

□ FOUR MONTHS BEFORE

Book flight tickets, tours or festivals,
organise necessary visas, and firm up
a version – in very broad strokes – of
what your itinerary might look like
(which days in which destination for
multi-stop trips). Start making
arrangements for ending your current
accommodation agreement if you're
renting, and storing your stuff
(or selling it).

□ TWO MONTHS BEFORE

Choose the right moment to
request time off work or to lodge
your resignation. Research your
first destination, book your first few
nights' accommodation, and where
you'll head to next. Check your
travel insurance (p47), back-up
option for accessing money (p28),
immunisations (p42), and teach
your grandma how to FaceTime.

□ ONE MONTH BEFORE

Once you begin the 30-day
countdown, you can take to your
social platforms to snoop for
upcoming events and fun places
to eat and drink, and even find
friends – or network with other
solo travellers – who might be
crisscrossing your itinerary.

THE SOLO TRAVEL QUIZ

Not sure where to start with your planning?
Take our quiz to reveal the type of trip that's right for you.

1. WHAT'S YOUR FAVOURITE STREET FOOD?

a) Deep-fried scorpions. Why not?
b) Tacos. Who doesn't love 'em?
c) Whatever everyone else is eating
d) Anything resembling a hot dog

2. WHAT'S YOUR BIGGEST SOLO TRAVEL FEAR?

a) Being bored
b) Getting lost
c) Eating alone
d) Losing your luggage

3. YOU'RE ON HOLIDAY. WHAT IS YOUR FOOTWEAR OF CHOICE?

a) Hiking boots
b) Nothing
c) Smart sandals
d) Heels

4. WHAT TYPE OF LUGGAGE DO YOU TAKE ON HOLIDAY?

a) A large rucksack, with space for a mosquito net and your snorkel
b) A small, lightweight rucksack that won't slow you down
c) Your big wheelie suitcase that you can't always manage
d) A small carry-on suitcase, so you don't have to check in

5. YOUR TRAVEL BUDDY ISN'T KEEN TO VISIT A MUSEUM YOU'VE BEEN DYING TO SEE. DO YOU:

a) Arrange to meet later and go by yourself
b) Go with the flow; you can always come back later
c) Get over it; stay with your pal
d) Convince them to wait for you while you have a quick look

6. WHAT'S YOUR IDEAL HOLIDAY WEATHER?

a) You don't mind as long as you can do the activities you want
b) Hot, hot, hot, with a cocktail on the side
c) Pleasant and sociable
d) Meh – you've packed for all possibilities

7. WHICH ACCESSORY WOULD MOST LIKELY BE FOUND IN YOUR CAR?

a) A sleeping bag, for spontaneous camping trips
b) A spare pair of sunglasses
c) An iPhone charger – you can't *not* be connected
d) Cash, in case of retail emergencies

8. WHAT'S YOUR FAVOURITE SOLO TRAVEL READ?

a) *Into the Wild* by Jon Krakauer
b) *The Beach* by Alex Garland
c) *On the Road* by Jack Kerouac
d) *The Sun Also Rises* by Ernest Hemingway

9. IN AN EMERGENCY, YOU'RE THE PERSON WHO TENDS TO:

a) Try to be a hero
b) Keep everyone calm
c) Recruit a bystander to help
d) Run! You've got places to be, anyway

10. YOU'RE HOSTING A DINNER PARTY. WHAT'S ON THE MENU?

a) An exotic curry you learnt to make on your last trip
b) Anything that can be cooked on a barbecue
c) Shared platters of finger food
d) Whatever you've ordered in

11. WHAT'S YOUR SPIRIT ANIMAL?

a) An elephant
b) A turtle
c) A meerkat
d) A dog

12. YOU HAVE A WEEK OFF AT HOME. WHAT DO YOU DO?

a) Take the opportunity to explore your own backyard
b) Grab a good book and position yourself next to a pool
c) Invite the gang around for drinks
d) Finally make that hair appointment

13. WHAT'S YOUR IDEA OF AN ADRENALIN RUSH?

a) Heli-skiing. Yee-haw!
b) Snorkelling
c) A rollercoaster ride
d) Running for the bus

14. WHAT KIND OF SOUVENIR ARE YOU LIKELY TO BRING BACK FROM A TRIP?

a) A tribal tattoo
b) The sand that you couldn't get out of your backpack
c) Lots of new Facebook friends
d) Jewellery

15. IT'S THE WEEKEND. WHAT ARE YOU DRINKING?

a) The weirdest-sounding craft beer the bar has on tap
b) Anything with an umbrella in it
c) You're sharing a bottle of red wine
d) Shots, baby – it's Saturday night!

16. YOUR FAVOURITE MODE OF PUBLIC TRANSPORT IS:

a) Rickshaws, simply because they're fun
b) Walking, because you prefer the fresh air
c) The bus, as it's easier to talk to people
d) The train, because it's gritty but quick

17. WHICH PLACE IS AT THE TOP OF YOUR SOLO TRAVEL BUCKET LIST?

a) Greenland, because I don't know anyone who has been there
b) Bali, because it sounds like a tropical paradise
c) Ireland, because I hear the locals are super-friendly
d) Paris, because... Paris

18. WHAT KIND OF CAMERA DO YOU TRAVEL WITH?

a) The latest GoPro
b) An iPhone, for the filters
c) A Polaroid-style camera, for group-picture fun
d) A digital SLR, for the quality

19. WHAT DO YOU MOST ENJOY DOING ALONE?

a) Taking a nice long hike somewhere
b) Going for a swim
c) Cooking for friends or family
d) Wandering around art galleries

20. WHAT'S YOUR IDEA OF A CULTURE SHOCK?

a) You're not easy to shock
b) The sights and smells of a local fish market
c) Travelling in a country where you don't speak the language
d) Bugs and leeches. Ew!

RESULTS
THIS WAY
⟫⟫⟶

THE SOLO TRAVEL HANDBOOK

RESULTS

MOSTLY AS
EMBARK ON A SOLO TRAVEL ADVENTURE

You can't help your insatiable curiosity of the world, so why not feed it? From trekking to ancient cities in South America (p101), to getting up close to the world's deadliest predators in Africa (p117), there are a million options. Just don't take off into the wilderness just yet. If it's your first big solo trip, opt for an achievable adventure – a trip that will satisfy your lust for adrenalin without putting your safety at risk. It's more important than ever to put some serious thought into your packing list for this trip; see p38 for tips.

MOSTLY BS
ESCAPE TO AN ISLAND PARADISE

Who says tropical island escapes are just for couples? There are loads of tropical islands around the world – from Caye Caulker in Belize (p132) to Ko Tao in Thailand – with huge solo traveller scenes. The beauty of an island holiday is that you can do as little or as much as you like. Use the trip as an opportunity to take that scuba diving course you've always wanted to, or simply enjoy the freedom to feel the sand between your toes, Instagram dazzling sunsets, and take siestas whenever you like.

MOSTLY CS
TAKE A SMALL GROUP TOUR

You like being around other people, and having your hand held – to a certain degree. Far from just an 'easy option', taking a group tour can often be the *best* option for nervous solo travellers who enjoy the comfort and safety of travelling in a group (p88), as well as the freedom to immerse yourself in the experience while somebody else manages your itinerary. Mealtimes are a particular highlight for solos who aren't fond of dining alone.

MOSTLY DS
GO FOR A CITY BREAK

For you, travel needs to be quick and easy. This is why solo city breaks suit you so well – you can enjoy new experiences with little chance of getting lonely (or needing to do your laundry), and you typically wear your everyday off-duty wardrobe, so packing is a cinch. Enjoy some alone time by staying in a hotel (perhaps splurging on room service), or save some cash and meet new people by choosing a hostel, and hit the town with your new friends. See p129 for the ultimate solo trip guide to Portland, USA.

© JUSTIN FOULKES / LONELY PLANET

© MATT MUNRO / LONELY PLANET

MONEY AND BUDGETING

Implementing a budget strategy and safeguarding your funds for use on the road is key in planning a seamless travel experience that won't put your financial future under unnecessary stress. Here's everything you need to know.

$ HOW MUCH MONEY WILL YOU REALLY NEED?

Once you've chosen your destination, do some online research to get a good grasp of how much money you are going to need to get by each day. Travel blogs are a great place to start – Gilles Barbier (grandescapades.net) publishes a cost breakdown of over 40 countries and regions he has travelled to, while Nick and Dariece Swift (goatsontheroad.com) offer cohesive cost breakdowns for Southeast Asian countries for couples and singles.

$ WHERE WILL YOU SLEEP?

If you're planning to travel on a shoestring, is budgeting for a dorm bed for every night of your trip realistic? If you're a light sleeper you may need to build in some extra funds to cover the cost of a private room every now and again.

$ WHERE WILL YOU EAT?

If you plan to get by on street food or standard local dishes, ensure this is going to be manageable for the duration of your trip – there is only so much fried rice most travellers can eat. Don't forget that some countries add significant taxes to the prices of restaurant food, such as the 'plus plus' system in Singapore.

$ WHAT ABOUT DRINKING?

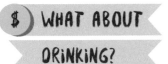

Don't forget to factor drinking costs in your dining budget. Whether your vice is coffee or craft beer, a single serving can cost as much as a meal – if not more – in some countries.

$ HOW WILL YOU GET AROUND?

It's important to have a good idea upfront of the type and cost of activities you wish to take part in on your trip, when planning your budget. If you're taking a small group tour, are there optional activities in the itinerary you may wish to do at an additional cost? If you are planning to scuba dive, how much will each dive cost? A fun dive in Indonesia can be as cheap as US$35, but you may pay triple that amount for a single dive in Australia.

$ WILL YOU DO ANY WORK WHILE TRAVELLING?

Doing some online work, or stopping somewhere to offer your skills in exchange for board, can take pressure off your travel funds, but it's not for everyone. Consider how much work your itinerary may allow for, and whether the amount you will earn or save will be worth the time you sacrifice to do it. See p69 for a guide to working on the road.

SETTING A BUDGET STRATEGY: THE 50/30/20 RULE REMASTERED

You may have heard of the 50/30/20 everyday budgeting rule, which suggests you allocate 50% of your income to essential costs (rent, bills, etc), allocate 30% to 'wants' (that new pair of shoes you've had your eye on), and allocate 20% to savings. When saving for a trip, this rule can be flipped to help you save more money, faster, says Bessie Hassan, money expert at international comparison website finder.com.

'There's no one-size-fits-all when setting a budget strategy, but allocating 50% of your earnings towards essential costs, 30% towards travel savings, and 20% for "wants" is a conservative approach that should see you grow your savings balance,' says Hassan. 'Putting greater emphasis on the percentage of earnings that go towards savings, and less emphasis on funds spent on "wants", is a tactical way to achieve your savings target.'

50% ESSENTIAL COSTS

30% WANTS

20% SAVINGS

↓ ↓ ↓

50% ESSENTIAL COSTS

30% TRAVEL SAVINGS

20% WANTS

$ HOW TO AVOID THE SOLO SURCHARGE

There are few worse insults to the solo traveller than being faced with the prospect of having to pay a single supplement when booking your trip. This dreaded surcharge – which can be as high as 100% – is imposed when one person occupies a room that is able to accommodate two, so you basically end up paying for your invisible companion. Avoid having to fork out for this cost by following these handy tips:

NEGOTIATE

TRAVEL IN THE LOW OR SHOULDER SEASON

BOOK WITH AN OPERATOR THAT SPECIALISES IN SINGLES HOLIDAYS

CONSIDER SHARING A ROOM

If you are booking at a time when the hotel or tour is unlikely to be sold out or is offering special deals, contact the operator to ask whether it will waive the single supplement – it just might.

You will have more bargaining power with hotels and operators outside the destination's high season, so give it your best shot. When hotel occupancy is low, operators are often more willing to give you a double room for the price of a single rather than miss out on filling the room altogether. Likewise for tours – if the tour isn't selling well, the operator may be willing to waive the single supplement for you.

These operators may offer the option of sharing a room with another solo traveller, or a room to yourself for little or no extra charge. As an added bonus, there is no risk of being forced to third-wheel, as your tour mates will also be solos. One drawback for younger travellers, however, is that many solo travel-specific operators are aimed at mature travellers. An exception is Exodus Travels (exodustravels.com), which offers solo departure dates for its most popular tours for travellers aged 16 and up.

Many operators offer to match you up with another traveller of the same sex to share a room. Best-case scenario, the operator isn't able to pair you up and you get a room all to yourself for no extra charge. More than half of passengers who travel with Intrepid Travel (intrepidtravel.com) and Contiki (contiki.com) are solo travellers, with both companies offering the option to match you up with a roomie. At the luxury end, Abercrombie & Kent (abercrombiekent.com) waives the solo supplement on selected journeys.

$) CASH, PLASTIC, TRAVELLER'S CHEQUES – HOW WILL YOU PAY?

It's all well and good to have a bunch of cash saved to travel, but it pays to organise your money for easy and secure access on the road. The more ways you are able to access your funds, the more flexibility you have if one source becomes unavailable – just be sure you know which source to use and when.

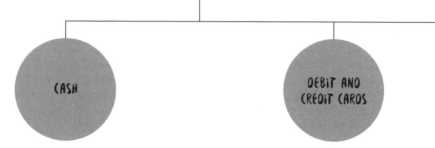

CASH

Travelling with a big wad of cash is always risky, but it can be handy to have an emergency stash of local currency (or easily exchangeable currency such as USD, the unofficial second currency of many countries) in small denominations up your sleeve. It is always cheaper to pre-order currency at home than use an ATM or money exchange bureau when you arrive, says Hassan.

'Bureau at airports are notorious for having less favourable rates because they are conveniently located and they know people need local currency fast, and they know people are less likely to compare their options,' Hassan says.

DEBIT AND CREDIT CARDS

Travelling with your regular debit and/or credit card might seem like a good option – especially if you earn air miles with purchases – but the costs of doing so can creep up.

'Cards can come with a series of fees,' says Hassan. 'Although it may be free to withdraw funds from an ATM, you may be charged a cash advance interest rate which means you'll pay around 20% interest from the time you withdraw the cash.

'Travellers should also be cautious of global transaction charges and international acceptance, as some cards won't be accepted in certain destinations,' Hassan adds. Look for cards that are part of a global ATM alliance network.

| FIVE THINGS TO DO BEFORE USING YOUR BANKCARD ABROAD | ★ Notify your bank of your travel plans so it doesn't cancel your card if it suspects suspicious activity. | ★ Set up direct debits so that you continue to meet your financial obligations on expenses. | ★ See how many interest-free days you have on your credit card to avoid late payment fees when home. | ★ Consider opening a linked account that no one can access if they get hold of your bank card. | ★ Ask your bank if it can supply an additional card for your account should your regular card get damaged. |

TOP TiP

'I'm a big fan of travel cards. You can pre-load them with a set amount, banks won't cut them off for irregular use, and you can often get a spare card to use as a back-up (I stash mine in my big pack), so if your wallet is lost or stolen, your financial loss is mitigated and there's a good chance you can still access the holiday cash remaining in the account with your back-up card.' NiCK HEWiTT, TRAVEL-MARKETiNG SPECiALiST

TRAVEL MONEY CARDS

TRAVELLER'S CHEQUES

Rather than relying solely on your everyday debit or credit card while travelling, consider using them in tandem with (or swapping them for) a travel money card that you can preload before you travel, and top up along the way

'Using a travel money card can be useful for savvy travellers who want to lock into a favourable exchange rate or avoid fees such as a currency conversion fee and ATM withdrawal fees,' says Hassan. Most travel money cards don't have raised numbers, which reduces the chance of your card being skimmed.

Hassan advises, however, to check for hidden costs before selecting a travel money card. 'When comparing prepaid travel money cards, keep an eye on the initial load fee, reload fees, ATM withdrawal fees that may apply, currency conversion fees and inactivity fees,' Hassan says. 'For instance, many of us don't realise you could be charged an inactivity fee if you don't use the card for 12 months after signing up for it, so make sure you read the terms and conditions. Lastly, if you're travelling to multiple destinations, remember to check that local currencies are supported by the card issuer.'

The global proliferation of ATMs has made traveller's cheques almost obsolete these days. They are no longer as widely accepted as they used to be, and exchanging them for cash can involve drawn-out bureaucracy and yards of red tape. However, they do have their advantages: they are accepted by banks and moneychangers all over the world and are easy to replace if lost or stolen. So long as you remembered to write down the serial numbers of the cheques and can track down the emergency phone number, you can get new cheques in a matter of days, though you may have to travel to a local agency to pick them up. Thomas Cook and American Express are the most widely accepted brands but, before you buy cheques, contact the issuer to find out just how widely they are accepted in your chosen destination, and which currency the cheques should be drawn in. When in doubt, carry cheques in US dollars. Bring a mix of denominations, and keep the receipts separate from the cheques.

10 GREAT WAYS TO SAVE MONEY TO TRAVEL

If you're really serious about saving money to travel, you will have to make some sacrifices – which isn't always easy or fun. That said, achieving your savings goal can be one of the most rewarding parts of the whole experience. That's because there really is nothing like sitting on a plane, about to start the journey of a lifetime, knowing that it was your own hard work that put you there.

Stephanie Parker, editor of budget travel blog bigworldsmallpockets.com, is an expert at putting herself in that plane seat. Here she shares her top 10 tips on making it your reality.

1) FIX YOUR FIGURES

When it comes to saving, having a clear financial goal is a great first step. To make the goal more manageable, divide it by the number of months (or even weeks) until your intended departure. Breaking down your savings goal like this will make it seem more attainable. You'll then have a clear idea of how much you need to save each time your pay cheque rolls in.

2) SIPHON OFF INTO A SAVER

Get an online savings account that accrues interest and give it a motivational name like 'I'm Outta Here!'. Keep your everyday account at a round number and siphon off any excess into your savings account. For example, if your account is at $34, transfer $4 into your savings. It's amazing how little you'll miss those few extra bucks, and it all adds up.

6) SELL YOUR STUFF

Getting rid of unwanted possessions can be a great way to save some cash. Join your local 'for sale' Facebook group, or use websites like ebay. com, craigslist.com and gumtree. com to sell books, clothes, furniture, exercise gear, and more. The more stuff you get rid of, the more money you can save on storage costs, too.

7) MAKE A NOTE OF IT

Taping a note to your bankcard that says something like 'do you want to travel or not?' is a great way to guilt yourself into restricting your spending. Every time you go to pay for something, you'll see the note and think twice.

3) PiGGY BANK iT

As well as topping up a savings account, get into a habit of putting high denomination coins straight into a piggy bank. Piggy banks that you have to smash to open are the best, as they remove the temptation to touch your savings too early.

4) CHANGE YOUR EATING HABiTS

When you consider that the cost of a single restaurant meal in New York, London or Sydney could keep you on the road in Nicaragua for several days, it makes sense to try to cut down on eating out. If you merely buy a sandwich every day, that's still up to $50 per week that could be going towards your savings. Sign up for supermarket newsletters so you can keep on top of promotions, and never shop when you're hungry!

5) REASSESS YOUR DRiNKiNG

If you can't manage cutting out alcohol, at least try to limit your consumption, and consider inviting friends over for drinks rather than meeting at a bar. And don't forget about coffee and smoothies. Just think, rather than spending $4 each day, you could make your own and save almost $2000 per year – that could keep you afloat for at least two months in Thailand. If you can't face giving up your cafe fix, an espresso typically costs less than half the price of a latte.

8) FiND THE FREE

Once you really commit to saving, you'll realise just how easy it is to seek out and enjoy things that are free. Most cities have free museums and galleries (or offer free entry on certain days of the month), while rural locations offer beach walks, waterfall swims and forest views, most of which can be enjoyed for nothing.

9) TAP iNTO THE SHARiNG ECONOMY

The sharing economy offers great ways to both save and make money. Perhaps you can cut costs down by signing up for a rideshare service like Lyft in the US (or a car share service like Car Next Door in Australia), or trade your old clothes for some travel gear you need at a clothes swap party? You could even add to your savings by spending a few hours each week assembling flat-pack furniture or distributing flyers via a sharing service like Airtasker.

10) REASSESS YOUR iNSURANCE

Could you be paying too much for health, car, or contents insurance? Check comparison websites to make sure you aren't getting a raw deal. While you're at it, you can compare travel insurance policies – you may be able to score a deal by bundling your insurance with the same provider.

THE SOLO TRAVEL HANDBOOK

BOOKiNG YOUR TRiP

So you've done your research, and you're ready to book that ticket! Before you start typing 'skyscanner.com' into your web browser or duck off to your travel agent, think about how much of your trip you actually need to book in advance. You may also be able to save some cash by booking your trip a certain way, or at a particular time.

HOW MUCH OF THE TRiP SHOULD YOU BOOK?

If you're planning a short trip, it makes sense to book a return flight, your accommodation, and any activities that may require pre-booking so you don't miss out, or waste time queuing for tickets and whatnot when you arrive. Be careful, however, not to overbook yourself – allow a buffer zone for spontaneous street food snacking, or heading out to a cool local bar with a group of travellers from your hostel.

If you have more flexibility with your return date, consider booking a one-way flight, or at least a return flight with the flexibility to change the return date or route. Booking at least one night's accommodation in a neighbourhood you anticipate spending a few days in takes the stress out of finding somewhere to stay when you arrive; booking two or three nights removes additional pressure to spend your first day in the destination hunting around for new accommodation if yours is fully booked for the following night.

HOW SHOULD YOU BOOK YOUR TRIP?

With hundreds of booking sites at your fingertips these days, travel agents might seem as obsolete as the printed map. But don't write them off just yet. Travel agents have access to special deals and software that the public don't, so they can often find cheaper flights and accommodation than you can track down yourself, with added bonuses like free meals and late check-out. Other benefits of booking through an agent include expert guidance, one-stop-shop convenience, and having someone on call to assist you if something unexpected happens during your holiday. That said, DIY booking can sometimes be cheaper, and often allows you the opportunity to scan travel options from a wider range of travel providers than agents work with. Shop around for the best deal.

WHEN SHOULD YOU BOOK IT?

It is commonly believed that the further in advance you book, the cheaper your trip will be. But this isn't always true. Most airline computers aren't programmed to offer deals earlier than six weeks before you wish to travel, so that 45-day mark is a good time to think about booking. Also consider the day on which you book – various studies have found that it is typically cheaper to book travel earlier in the week, and cheaper to fly on certain days (see p35). Signing up for travel newsletters also gives you an opportunity to book deals you may not come across otherwise.

10 OF THE BEST FLIGHT-BOOKING HACKS

Former NGO director Clint Johnston flies for free, and never pays full price for travel. He shares the tips and tricks he has learned while travel hacking his way around more than 100 countries at triphackr.com, which Johnston now runs full-time. Here he reveals his top 10 flight-booking hacks.

1 BOOK AT THE RIGHT TIME

Knowing when to purchase a flight is key to finding the cheapest deals. According to various studies, the magic number ranges from 47 to 60 days before your departure date on international flights. Airfares fluctuate constantly and there is no need to wait to book a flight in hopes of a fare continuing to drop. Book your flight in the booking sweet spot for the best deal.

2 FLY INTO ALTERNATIVE AIRPORTS

Major airports are often located nearby other airports and you can take advantage of this to save money on your flight. For example, instead of flying into Los Angeles, California, check nearby airports that are only a short drive away. Alternative airports near LA include Long Beach, Burbank, Ontario, and John Wayne, which are all within 80km (50 miles).

6 JOIN FREQUENT FLYER PROGRAMMES AND EARN MILES

If you aren't already signed up for frequent flyer programmes, consider doing so. There are three main global airline alliances where miles can be transferred between airlines. This means if you fly on Delta you can redeem miles on KLM since they are both part of the SkyTeam Alliance. Never let a mile go to waste, even if flying with an airline for the first time.

7 SET UP FARE ALERTS TO TRACK FLIGHTS

Before you ever book you should start tracking it 2-3 months before your departure date. For example, if the booking sweet spot is 47-60 days before the departure date you should set up your fare alerts 90 days before a flight. If the flight happens to drop to a very low price they will email you and you can book it early. Use sites such as Kayak and Skyscanner to set up fare alerts.

3 BOOK A LAYOVER THAT IS ACTUALLY YOUR END DESTINATION

Airlines aren't keen on this but it saves money. Sites like Skiplagged will help you find hidden city fares. If you're flying from London to Istanbul, Skiplagged will find you a flight to a final destination with a layover in Istanbul. Instead of continuing on, you will exit the airport in Istanbul, which was your final stop all along. Just don't check any bags!

4 TAKE ADVANTAGE OF FLIGHT DEALS AND ERROR FARES

If you are flexible with your travel dates, you can book ultra-low fares. Sites such as theflightdeal.com and travelpirates.com constantly search for the best deals available and share them across their social channels. Error fares occur often and most airlines will honour these error prices. Make sure to book quickly as they don't last long.

5 SIGN UP FOR NEWSLETTERS TO BOOK CHEAP FLIGHTS

Sign up for newsletters from all the major airlines. Newsletters are a great way to stay on top of the cheapest fares and ways to earn miles and points from each airline.

8 BOOK BY THE FARE INSTEAD OF THE DESTINATION

If you want to travel but are not set on the destination, you should search by the lowest fare. Kayak offers the 'explore' tool and Skyscanner allows you to search 'everywhere' by month, which shows you the lowest fares around the world for a particular region. For example, if your plan was to travel to more than one country in Europe then there is no need to focus your flight on one city when you can simply fly into the cheaper region to start your trip.

9 USE HISTORICAL DATA TO KNOW WHEN TO BOOK

Kayak offers a historical pricing tool called 'price forecast'. This tool will show you if a flight is likely to rise or fall within the next seven days using historical data. If the current fare is high, the tool may advise you to wait but if it is low, it will tell you to book now.

10 FLY ON TUESDAYS, WEDNESDAYS, AND SATURDAYS

Flying on unpopular days is one of the easiest ways to save money on a flight. Everybody wants to fly on a Friday or Sunday and few people want to interrupt their weekend by flying on Saturday. Airlines need to fill these unpopular seats on flights mid-week and you can use this to your advantage.

LUGGAGE AND PACKING

All savvy travellers know that your luggage and packing choices have the potential to make or break a trip. For solo travellers, it's even more crucial to nail it, as you can't bank on having someone else around to help carry your luggage, or lend you an essential travel item you may have forgotten to pack yourself. Follow these steps and you'll never need to rely on a travel sidekick again.

THE VESSEL: CHOOSING YOUR LUGGAGE

When choosing luggage, first consider your destination and the type of travel you plan on doing. If it's backpacking around India, your trusty wheelie suitcase isn't going to cut it; if you're jetting away for a quick city break, your big old dusty backpack probably isn't ideal.

Whatever type of luggage you choose, opt for lightweight and inconspicuous – designer luggage may make you more vulnerable to thieves. Don't just consider cabin baggage size and weight restrictions when purchasing luggage, but also the weight you are comfortable carrying. If you've narrowed a new purchase down to several options, opt for the one with with the best warranty.

HOW TO CHOOSE A SUITCASE

★ Look for a suitcase with spinner wheels, which makes your bag much easier to control.
★ Ensure the zips are sturdy and lockable. Some travellers swear by inbuilt suitcase locks, though these can sometimes jam.
★ Weigh up the benefits of a hard versus soft case: hard suitcases can be lighter, but they don't absorb shock as well as soft cases; the latter can also fit more easily into overhead storage lockers in planes.
★ If opting for a soft case, look for a case with an exterior (ideally lockable) pocket for a pair of flip-flops or change of clothes for a quick post-flight change.
★ Pricier cases might look snazzier and have more features, but after being tossed around, they are often just as likely to break as cheaper cases.

HOW TO CHOOSE A BACKPACK

★ Keep your eye out for backpacks that have a front rather than top opening, so you don't have to take empty your bag every time you need something, and a waist strap to distribute weight more evenly.
★ If the straps on the pack you wish to purchase are adjustable, ask the store person to fit them for you so you get the best support.
★ Opt for a pack with a zip-off daypack that doubles up as a carry-on if you're planning to travel light.
★ Ensure the pack has an inbuilt cover for the back straps that you can zip on for travel so the straps don't get caught in luggage conveyer belts.
★ It's worthwhile investing in a good-quality backpack designed for adventure travel, as cheaper varieties are less likely to have sturdy straps and good back support.

WHAT ABOUT DUFFEL BAGS?

★ Increasingly popular duffel bags are large, cylindrical and mostly made of soft fabric.
★ They provide easy access to the bag's hollow cylindrical interior, and you can squish the bag into a tight spot.
★ Some come with shoulder straps, but these don't offer great back support.

HOW TO PACK LIKE A PRO

Save time, space and your sanity with these handy tips.

USE THE CLEVER PACKPOINT APP TO CREATE A BESPOKE PACKING LIST, AND STICK TO IT SO YOU CAN BE SURE YOU'VE GOT THE ESSENTIALS COVERED.

Do a trial pack before your trip to make sure everything will fit, and re-pack the day before you go after checking the weather forecast, and adjusting your packing list accordingly.

Opt for quick-drying garments that don't require ironing. Natural materials such as bamboo, cotton, cashmere and wool have a low-wrinkle factor (though the latter two can take more time to dry). Synthetic materials including polyester, Lyocell and Lycra are also crush-resistant, and tend to dry more quickly.

To prevent make-up palettes cracking, place a cotton wool bud between the shadow and palette lid.

EMBRACE CLEAR PACKING CUBES, WHICH MAKE IT EASIER FOR YOU TO FIND YOUR STUFF IN YOUR BAG, KEEP CLEAN GARMENTS FRESH, AND DIRTY CLOTHES OR SHOES ISOLATED.

NEVER PACK UNWORN SHOES, WHICH HAVE THE POTENTIAL TO LAND YOU IN BLISTER HELL.

Unless you will have no access to washing facilities (such as a hotel sink) on your trip, don't pack more than a week's worth of underwear. Disposable underwear is not environmentally sound, so it's not an ideal back-up.

TIE A COLOURFUL RIBBON, BAG STRAP OR ANOTHER IDENTIFYING MARKER TO THE OUTSIDE OF YOUR BAG TO PREVENT SOMEONE WITH THE SAME TYPE OF LUGGAGE GRABBING YOURS BY MISTAKE (IT HAPPENS). ALWAYS ENSURE YOUR LUGGAGE IS CLEARLY LABELLED WITH YOUR NAME AND CONTACT DETAILS.

Pack heavy things like shoes at the bottom of your luggage, so it doesn't topple over when standing stationary.

Decant your toiletries into mini reusable bottles (ideally twist tops, which have a lower blow-out factor than the pop-top variety). Pack these, and other items such as toothpaste, in reusable zip-lock bags.

ALL HAIL THE CARRY-ON

Many rookie travellers underestimate the importance of having a good-quality, well-packed carry-on bag. Embracing your carry-on not only lowers the risk of your valuables disappearing from your suitcase, but it can also get you out of a jam in a mid-flight seatmate snoring emergency, or – heaven forbid – when your checked luggage doesn't arrive with you. Most airline carry-on weight restrictions will allow you to cram in the essentials, including:

© STYF22 / GETTY IMAGES

ALL YOUR VALUABLES.
If this makes your bag too heavy, consider wearing your valuables on the plane, or leave some of them at home.

A scarf.
A DARK-COLOURED OR PATTERNED PASHMINA MAKES THE PERFECT BLANKET THAT WILL ALSO HIDE IN-FLIGHT SPILLS.

AN OVERNIGHT KIT.
Include earplugs and an eye mask, as these are no longer complimentary for economy passengers on many airlines.

Compression socks.
WEARING THESE ON LONGER FLIGHTS DOESN'T JUST DECREASE YOUR RISK OF DEEP VEIN THROMBOSIS, BUT ALSO DECREASES THE RISK OF DEVELOPING SPIDER AND VARICOSE VEINS.

READING MATERIAL.
Or a journal to doodle in if you get bored or delayed.

A full change of clothes.
PLUS A COUPLE OF DAYS' SUPPLY OF ANY IMPORTANT MEDICATIONS, AND ANY ESSENTIAL ITEMS YOU WILL NEED FOR THE DESTINATION SUCH AS SWIMWEAR.

REUSABLE WATER BOTTLE.
Pack an empty bottle that you can fill at the airport after you pass through security to ensure you always have access to hydration during your journey. S'well bottles (swellbottle.com) and Earth Eco Bottles (theseeksociety.com) keep water cold for 24 hours!

ESSENTIAL TOILETRIES.
Pack deodorant, mouthwash or a travel toothbrush and toothpaste, moisturiser, tissues and paw-paw ointment or lip balm. You may also wish to bring face wipes and a hydrating foundation for a pre-arrival pep-up.

14 ITEMS EVERY SOLO WORLD TRAVELLER SHOULD CARRY WITH THEM

Complemented by a well-stocked first-aid kit (p45), these travel aids will help you navigate solo travel like a pro.

1. GOOD-QUALITY HEAD TORCH

Don't be *that guy* who turns on the light in a hotel dorm at 3am because you didn't pack a head torch. Head torches are especially handy on multi-day treks when you won't have access to electricity at night, but shouldn't be dismissed by higher-end travellers, who may find themselves needing one when hotel room lighting is poor.

2. UNLOCKED SMARTPHONE

Having a local SIM card can make your life on the road a lot easier, while providing an extra degree of connectivity and safety for solo travellers. But you can't use one, or do much with it, unless you have an unlocked smartphone.

3. UTILITY KNIFE

A utility knife can be used for everything from cutting up local fruit for lunch to filing your nails; trimming frayed clothes to tightening up a loose screw in your glasses. Just remember to pack it in your checked luggage.

4. PLASTIC AND CANVAS BAGS

A stash of plastic bags – especially zip-lock bags and packing cubes – can come in very handy, as they can be used for everything from makeshift laundry baskets to emergency raincoats. Better yet, substitute as much plastic as you can for more eco-friendly reusable lightweight cloth bags.

5. SARONG

A sarong can be used in multiple ways, from a headscarf to a beach towel; a sleeping sheet to a protective wrap for a fragile travel souvenir. Better yet, sarongs are cheap and available everywhere.

6. TRAVEL TOWEL

If you're not keen to use your sarong as a bath towel, pack a quick-drying travel towel for those occasions when towel rental is not included in hostel rates, which can be more common than you might think.

7. UNIVERSAL ADAPTOR

Eliminate the possibility of getting caught out by foreign power sockets; some countries use several types.

8. POWER PACK

Handy for juicing your phone or camera battery on the go when you are travelling without access to a power source.

9. RAIN PONCHO OR GARBAGE BAG

If you're not headed to an especially rainy destination, switch your bulky umbrella for a lightweight rain poncho you can whip out if the skies open. Garbage bags make great backpack raincoats.

10. FLIP-FLOPS

Even if you're not headed to a beachy destination, flip-flops can come in handy for visiting spas, protecting your feet from communal shower nasties, or simply giving hiking boot-confined feet a break.

11. PACKING SCALE

Avoid airport repacking scrambles and excess baggage fees by knowing exactly how much your bag weighs before you check it in. Newer travel scale models are quite lightweight, so you can keep the scale in your bag while you travel.

TOP TIP

'I always pack a few three-quarter-length skirts and some T-shirts that cover my shoulders. I've visited a lot of places where the culture is more conservative than I am used to. Being respectful of the local culture – especially in religious sites – can go a long way. It also helps avoid potentially dangerous situations in regions where women showing too much skin might be harassed.' *PHOEBE LEE, TRAVEL BLOGGER, LITTLEGREYBOX.NET*

12. TRAVEL PILLOW

On a long trip, your neck is going to want one of these. Choose an inflatable version, so you don't have to find space to stash a bulky plush pillow.

13. TOILET PAPER

An emergency loo roll may very well get you out of a potentially sticky situation, especially if you are travelling to a developing country.

14. A ROLL OF DUCT TAPE

Handy for using as a temporary fix for luggage tears, broken sunglasses frames or holes in shoes. Can also be used to make a splint, protect against blisters, make a sink plug, seal food containers, and more.

PRE-TRIP HEALTH

It's no fun getting sick when you're travelling by yourself. But with a bit of preparation, you can protect yourself from the usual health hazards. And ensure you have read the fine print on your travel insurance.

WHAT IMMUNISATIONS WILL I NEED?

'Immunisations fall into three categories: routine, recommended and required, and these vary for every destination,' says Dr Deborah 'Deb' Mills, travel doctor and author of travel health bible Travelling Well. Dr Deb recommends visiting a travel health doctor six to eight weeks before your trip to ensure you have time to get the vaccinations you may need, as some (including Hepatitis A and Japanese Encephalitis) require several jabs over a period of time. Yellow fever is the most commonly required vaccination for travelling abroad, requiring you to present your vaccination card upon your return (or when entering any country that requires this card) if you have travelled to an affected region.

WHAT ABOUT THE NASTIES THAT CAN'T BE VACCINATED AGAINST?

At the time this book went to print, there were exciting things happening in the world of travel medicine – a dengue fever vaccine had been launched in the Philippines, an Ebola vaccine had been successfully trialled in Guinea, and human trials for the Zika virus vaccine had kicked off in the US. Malaria rates are also dropping around the world. This doesn't mean, however, that travellers should be complacent.

'It's important to do your research so you know what the health hazards are in the destination you are travelling to, and how to protect yourself,' says Dr Deb. 'If mosquito-borne diseases are a risk, layer up with a heavy-duty insect repellent like DEET or Picaridin. If methanol poisoning is an issue, stick to drinking beer and avoid spirits.'

Dr Deb also advises assessing the risks in the specific region you will be travelling to, rather than the whole country. 'Malaria is a risk in parts of Vietnam, but if you are simply doing a food tour in Hanoi, you may not need malaria medication. You can also protect yourself from other nasties by being conscious of your personal hygiene. 'If you can't drink the tap water, don't wash your toothbrush with it either,' says Dr Deb.

THE RABIES VACCINE: TO GET IT OR NOT?

The vaccine for rabies – a fatal disease transmitted by saliva, usually from dogs – is a dilemma for many travellers, with many choosing to opt out of the three (often expensive) injections of the vaccine required before travelling. If you are travelling to an affected area, this is a huge risk, says Dr Deb.

'If you didn't get the vaccine and you get bitten by an infected animal, you need to get the first of up to five doses of the vaccine, as well as an injection of Rabies Immune Globulin into the wound, as soon as possible – ideally within 24 hours – or you will die. If you had the vaccine and you get bitten, you will only need two booster shots of the vaccine, and you have a bit more time to access treatment – the average person takes about four days to access the booster vaccine,' she says.

The rabies vaccine is typically recommended to people who are likely to be travelling to high-risk areas (most of Asia and Africa), and those who plan to handle animals (on a volunteer project, for example), but plenty of travellers who make a conscious effort to stay away from animals get bitten – a 2012 study found at least one out of every hundred travellers to Southeast Asia was bitten by an animal.

'Most cases I see involve the patient surprising the animal,' says Dr Deb. 'In one case a boy was bitten by a dog he didn't see under a restaurant table, while other people have been bitten while getting out of taxis.' It's not always obvious if an animal is infected, so take every precaution if bitten.

WHAT MEDICATIONS SHOULD I BRING?

Dr Deb recommends packing any medications you typically use at home (from contraceptives to asthma medication), as well as destination- and travel-style-specific medication advised by your doctor. 'This could include medication to treat everything from malaria to altitude sickness, travel sickness to diarrhoea,' says Dr Deb.

TOP TIP

'Never assume personal health products you can easily buy in your home country will be readily available abroad. Suncream is notoriously hard to find, and when you do find it, it can be horrendously expensive, and lack the UV protection required for the destination. I also always travel with a stash of tampons, which can be similarly difficult to find in some countries.' RIA DE JONG, LONELY PLANET WRITER

DON'T FORGET YOUR TEETH

'If you'll be travelling for a while, making an appointment to see your dentist before you go is a good idea, as dental problems can be difficult and expensive to treat while travelling,' says Dr Deb. If you're due for any other check-ups, such as a smear test or an eye check, knocking these off before you go could literally save you a lot of pain.

FIRST AID KIT ESSENTIALS

'A good first aid kit will include the essentials to treat the four most common travel ailments: gastro intestinal illnesses, chest infections, pain and wounds,' says Dr Deb. Have the confidence to treat minor travel nasties by packing the following items in your kit:

+ ANTIHISTAMINES
+ ANTISEPTIC WIPES OR CREAM
+ ANTIBIOTIC OINTMENT
+ BANDAGE
+ DESTINATION- AND TRIP-STYLE-
  SPECIFIC MEDICATIONS (SEE P44)
+ EAR BUDS/Q-TIPS
+ FLU MEDICATION AND THROAT
  LOZENGES
+ HAND SANITISER
+ INSECT REPELLENT (DEET OR PICARDIN)

+ MICROPORE TAPE
+ NAIL SCISSORS AND TWEEZERS
+ ORAL REHYDRATION SALTS
+ PARACETAMOL OR IBUPROFEN
+ SPORTS STRAPPING TAPE
+ STERI-STRIPS
+ STICKY PLASTERS OF DIFFERENT SIZES
  (INCLUDING BLISTER PLASTERS)
+ SAFETY PINS
+ SUNSCREEN (AT LEAST 30+)
+ TOPICAL ANTIBIOTIC OINTMENT

TYING UP LOOSE ENDS

Whether you're heading off on a short trip or long journey, there are important steps to take to ensure both a smooth transition to the real world upon your return, and the safety and security of your possessions while you are travelling.

At work

Planning to resign from your job to travel? Don't leave it until the last minute to hand in your notice, which could risk your chance of securing a great reference. If you're simply taking annual leave, ensure your leave is signed off by your manager in advance and you hand over any unfinished projects to colleagues in good time.

Ensure your out-of-office message contains details of the most appropriate member of staff that can be contacted in your absence. Before turning it on and shutting down your computer on your last day (wahoo!), double-check your calendar to ensure you have responded to any meeting or event invitations that require an RSVP before your return.

At home

If you plan to rent out or sublet your home while you're away, ensure you have a contingency plan, anything from leaving a list of contacts for trusted tradesmen, to enlisting a friend or rental agent who can manage any issues on your behalf. If you don't share your living space with anyone else and you plan to leave it empty, entrust a friend or family member to check in on your place, being sure to empty your mailbox or turn on your heating periodically to prevent pipes cracking.

Secure your valuables and, if you have contents insurance, ensure it is still valid if you temporarily store things elsewhere.

And to minimise the risk of a break-in, invest in some electronic timer switches.

Your stuff

If you are moving out of a flatshare or need to move your things out of your own home to make room for a tenant, ask yourself whether it will be better to store or sell your stuff – storage fees can stack up quickly, and if you're away for a long time, you might return to find you no longer want much of the stuff you stored. Having lockable storage installed in your home is another option that might end up being cheaper (and less time consuming) than using a storage company.

Don't forget to wind down your grocery shop in the weeks leading up until your trip, making use of existing pantry items rather than buying more food that might spoil while you are away.

TOP TIP

'Are you planning to drive overseas? First make sure you renew your drivers' licence if it is nearing expiry. Also find out before you leave home if you'll need an International Driving Permit (IDP). Not all countries require these, but many do. The IDP is recognised as valid identification in over 150 countries as well, so you don't have to risk taking your passport out to a bar to be able to buy a drink.'

TASMIN WABY, LONELY PLANET
DESTINATION EDITOR

Personal matters

Before you go, pay your bills and ensure your financial obligations are in order. If you are not able to use your mobile (cell) phone plan overseas, consider suspending or cancelling your plan. It's also a good idea to put any memberships and subscriptions on hold, as well as health insurance if yours is not valid overseas.

When travelling solo, let the people close to you know where and when you are going, and how they can reach you. Entrust at least one person with copies of all your travel documents (passport, ID, insurance details, travel bookings, copies of bankcards), plus confirm all your bookings again while you're at it. Additionally, let government agencies know you're away.

ON THE ROAD

ARRIViNG iN YOUR DESTiNATiON

Stepping off a plane, boat, bus or train in a new destination – let alone by yourself – has the tendency to trigger a variety of emotions, from an adrenalin rush of excitement through to feelings of sheer terror. Planning ahead for this moment will give you the confidence to revel in the thrill of it, while keeping a cool head.

HOW TO ARRiVE iN ANY NEW DESTiNATiON LiKE A BOSS

★ Plan to arrive in daylight hours: it's typically safer and lowers the risk of airport transport services being unavailable.

★ Have your first night's accommodation booked, or at least know which neighbourhood you wish to stay in, and either pre-book a transfer, or research how to get there by other means in advance, as well as how much it should cost.

★ Bring a map of the area your accommodation is located in, or download one on your phone so you can access it if you don't have wi-fi on arrival.

★ When the pilot or conductor announces the local time in your destination, reset your watch so you aren't tempted to fiddle with it in the arrivals hall when you should be keeping an eye on your belongings.

★ Research local customs and check the weather before you depart, and have an easily accessible change of clothes handy that you can throw on in the arrivals hall, or when you arrive at your accommodation, so you don't have to rummage through your suitcase in public if you can't check in straight away.

★ Preload your destination's currency exchange rate into your phone (try the XE Currency App, which can be used offline) in case you can't get wi-fi at your destination, so you aren't left fumbling (or worse – guessing) at the ATM.

★ If you didn't bring any local currency with you, use an airport ATM or currency exchange counter to obtain enough local currency to get you by for a day or two so you won't be forced to use your card for small purchases, or find yourself in a tight spot if your card isn't accepted.

★ Ignore offers from strangers to help with your bags (unless you really need it, and then only from official staff who are happy to show you their ID).

★ Keep a sharp eye on your belongings – if your bag is to be loaded onto a shuttle bus, don't take your seat until you see your bag loaded in the vehicle.

★ Be extremely wary of offers from strangers to share a taxi. You've seen *Taken*, right?

★ Scope out the terminal layout and amenities, so you know what to expect if you are planning to depart from the same airport.

★ If you need a local SIM card, consider purchasing one in the arrivals hall so this task doesn't eat into your holiday time the following day.

★ Research food outlets near your accommodation before you travel, so you don't have to spend time doing this research when you arrive hungry (or worse – hangry).

★ When checking in to your accommodation, ask staff to mark on a map where it is safe (or otherwise) to wander around solo. Don't be shy to ask for dining tips, too – they may know of a new convenient spot that isn't in your guidebook.

★ When you are settled into your accommodation, alert a friend or family member that you have arrived safely, and let them know how to get in touch with you if they need to.

★ If it's still daylight, head outside – it helps your body calibrate to the local time zone. And try to stay awake until your usual bedtime. Even if you're travelling in the same zone, getting out and about helps to refresh and re-energise.

★ Take pictures. Some photographers say that their eyes are 'freshest' when they first arrive in a new place – you may notice things in the first few hours that you unconsciously ignore after a day or two.

MANAGING YOUR MONEY

It's the ultimate travel nightmare: you use an ATM in a remote part of the world and it eats your card. What do you do? All you have left in your pocket is a few notes and there's still the hotel bill to pay. You could always throw yourself on the mercy of strangers, but it's best to have a plan B, particularly when it comes to your hard-earned travel cash. It's crucial to prepare for worst-case scenarios before you leave home – it's much less stressful than trying to troubleshoot in a foreign country. Here's how to keep your money flowing – and safe – on the road.

CARRYING CASH

The golden rule for travel money is never keep all your eggs (money) in one basket (the same bag or wallet). If you get robbed or misplace your stuff, you lose everything. Carry a useful amount of cash for a day hidden somewhere discreet, and leave the rest in a secure spot, like your hotel safe, even if you plan to primarily use a bankcard while abroad. Everyone has his or her own trick for hiding emergency stash: money belts, secret pockets, a Ziploc bag tucked into the lining of your suitcase, an old film canister in your washbag. Here are some more handy tips for how to handle cash when you're on the road:

★ US dollars, British pounds and Euros are the easiest currencies to change, particularly in the developing world. Keep enough aside to support yourself for several days. Use smaller-denomination bills, so you don't have to change everything at a disadvantageous rate.

★ Changing money on the street is a great way to get ripped off – especially if you're unfamiliar with the local currency. Always be sure to exchange foreign currency with a recognised trader, such as a bank or exchange bureau.

★ Ignore boasts of 'no commission' as this won't always mean you get more bang for your buck. Do your research and find out exactly how much money you'll get from the exchange – the more you get, the better the deal.

© ROBERTO WESTBROOK / GETTY IMAGES

TOP TIP

'There are some destinations where cash is still the only game in town, so if you're travelling to one of them, ensure you have enough. Parts of Africa and Asia have yet to plug into the global ATM network (and many US-issued cards still don't work in Cuba), so the only money available is what you bring in. Even some of the world's most developed countries – like Germany and Japan – continue to maintain a cash-based economy, with many businesses refusing to accept cards.' SARAH REID, TRAVEL WRITER

USING CARDS

It's smart to have a mix of these so that you have back-up if your primary money goes missing. Here are a few tips for using them on the road:

★
Bring multiple cards and store your extra cards locked away in your room's safe with your other valuables, in case of emergencies.

★
Don't forget to factor in bank charges – most banks charge a fee for every withdrawal, and most offer poor exchange rates for credit and debit cards.

★
If you have the option, pay in the local currency on your debit or credit card when abroad, as your bank's rates will be better than the retailer's.

★
Keep essential emergency phone numbers handy – that means the local police and the international number to cancel your cards if need be.

★
Never let your card out of your sight. Most credit card scams require time alone with your card – if you don't see an electronic point-of-sale machine, play it safe and pay with cash from an ATM.

★
Check the layout of the keypad on the ATM. Loads of travellers lose their cards by entering the right pattern but the wrong numbers on a foreign ATM keypad.

★
On top of having a back-up card, don't forget back-up cash or traveller's cheques. ATMs rely on electricity supply and a phone signal, things that are notoriously unreliable in the developing world.

MAXIMISING TRAVELLER'S CHEQUES

If you've decided to bring some traveller's cheques as a back-up, use them wisely. Essentially, this means cashing in your larger-denomination cheques when you'll be in town for a while, saving the smaller-denomination cheques for the end of your trip. Local businesses that change cheques will invariably always offer a lower rate than a proper agency. The rate is typically even lower if you use a traveller's cheque to pay for a purchase directly, so try to avoid it.

WIRING MONEY

If all other options fail, you could always ask a generous friend or family member at home to wire you money. Western Union and Moneygram have agents all over the world where you can receive a wire transfer from home, but you pay a premium for the service – sometimes as much as 30% of the transfer amount.

4 GREAT APPS FOR MANAGING TRAVEL MONEY

XE

With 40 million downloads and counting, XE is the world's most downloaded currency exchange app. The free app also functions offline by saving the last updated rates for currencies you have preloaded (up to 10), which is especially convenient for those times when you arrive in a new destination and need to withdraw or exchange cash, but you don't have an internet connection to check the market rates.

MINT

This personal finance app gives you a real-time, complete look into all of your finances, from bank accounts and credit cards, to student loans and pension funds. It automatically tracks your spending, categorises it, and alerts you when/if you approach your budget limit. You can even ask for custom savings tips within the app. It only links to US and Canadian financial institutions, but there are similar versions for other countries, such as Pocketbook in Australia, and OnTrees in the UK.

TRAIL WALLET

Designed by the couple behind travel blog neverendingvoyage.com, this nifty app allows you to organise your expenses by trip or by month, set yourself a daily budget, then add expenses as you go. Simply launch the app, punch in an expense using the 'quick add' screen, and you're done. At the end of the day, week, or month, you can check the summary screen to see how you're doing.

SPLITTR

If you hook up with other travellers on your journey and find yourself needing to split bills, Splittr provides a simple platform to share costs. You can enter expenses as you go, including who paid what, and the app will do the rest. Handily for overseas trips, all currencies are supported – and you can mix currencies without having to do the conversion yourself.

TOP TIP

'If you're looking for cheap accommodation on the fly, search for the rate online but don't book. Then walk into the hostel or hotel and ask if they have any vacancies – you know they do because minutes ago you could still book online. Ask if they have a cheap room and you will usually be offered a room at a lower rate than available online. This handy discount is possible when the accommodation provider doesn't have to pay the booking site a commission fee.' JACKSON GROVES, TRAVEL BLOGGER, JOURNEYERA.COM

ACCOMMODATION

Accommodation is usually the biggest daily expense. Lowering its cost can give you more flexibility with funds. However, safety and security are vital when choosing somewhere to stay.

7 TIPS FOR SAVING MONEY ON ACCOMMODATION

1 Call the hotel in advance to ask if staff can offer a better rate than the one advertised. They may offer you a discount.

2 Look for three-night-stay deals and be flexible with your dates.

3 Look for accommodation with kitchens for guest use so you can cook a cheap meal in when you don't feel like going out.

4 If you plan to stick around for a while, ask if the hostel offers free board in exchange for a few hours' work each day.

5 Opt to stay with a local for free via websites like couchsurfing.com.

6 Accommodation rentals are often cheaper than hotels, and sometimes even hostels. The most well known is airbnb.com, but there are plenty of other options including roomorama.com and wimdu.com.

7 Check several sites before booking you might be surprised how much prices can fluctuate. In Asia, agoda.com is the best hotel-booking site for the region.

8 QUESTIONS TO ASK BEFORE BOOKING ACCOMMODATION

1. WHAT HAVE PAST GUESTS SAID ABOUT THE PLACE?
Online reviews should always be taken with a grain of salt, but generally they provide a decent overview of the property and service.

2. IS THE LOCATION OF THE ACCOMMODATION PRACTICAL AND SAFE?
Having to walk 10 blocks in a dodgy area to reach the closest public transport hub is not ideal.

3. WHAT IS THE CHECK-IN AND CHECK-OUT TIME?
If you will be arriving early or departing after check-out, ensure the accommodation can store your luggage for you so you don't have to lug it around.

4. WHAT SECURITY FEATURES DOES IT OFFER?
All good hostels have personal lockers.

5. DOES IT OFFER FREE WI-FI, AND WHERE?
Some places only offer wi-fi in the lobby. Check online reviews to help get a sense whether the connection at your intended accommodation is reliable.

6. ARE THERE ANY HIDDEN FEES?
Check if the accommodation requires additional fees or taxes to be paid.

7. IS BREAKFAST INCLUDED OR ARE COOKING FACILITIES AVAILABLE?
If not, make sure there is a cafe or supermarket close by where you can grab snacks easily.

8. IS THERE A CURFEW?
This could pose a problem if you plan to arrive or stay out late.

HOSTEL SURVIVAL SKILLS 101

Offering cheap accommodation and golden opportunities to meet other travellers, hostels can be a solo traveller's best friend. But not all hostels were created equal. Follow these steps to get the best out of your hostel experience.

Embrace the hostel cafe. There is no shame in eating at your hostel if you don't feel like going out by yourself once in a while – some hostels have great, affordable menus.

Observe hostel etiquette. Keen to make friends? Keep your voice down and don't turn on the main light in a dorm between around 10pm and 8am, keep your belongings contained, clean up after yourself, and book a private room if you snore.

Choose your bed wisely. If you are given a choice, opt for a bed away from the door and bathroom to limit your chances of being woken up at night, yet near a power point. The bottom bunk usually offers easier access to your bag, though the top bunk can sometimes feel more private.

Check for bedbugs. Pull back the sheets to check for small dark spots (bed bug excrement) on the mattress, yellow eggs and eggshells, as well as the tiny bugs, which are often found in mattress seams, behind headboards and in electrical sockets.

Use your locker. If security lockers are provided, use them (ideally with your own padlock). If not, ask the manager if you can leave valuables in their safe. No matter how friendly your roommates seem, some travellers (and accommodation staff) have ulterior motives.

Opt for a dorm away from the hostel common area, and with as few beds as possible. Some hostels charge the same rate for all dorms, no matter how many beds they contain. Unless you're a heavy sleeper, more dorm-mates mean a higher chance of late-night interruptions.

Do your research. Read online reviews to ensure the hostel you wish to book appears to meet your needs. Be wary of hostels with no reviews, or a high proportion of negative reviews.

Keep an overnight kit under your pillow. Keep a little pouch containing earplugs, an eye mask and a head torch within easy reach at night.

Be on time for breakfast. Some hostels that offer an included breakfast provide a limited quota of food every day that may run out if you don't get in early.

Note the emergency exit. Some hostels maximise space by jamming beds up against emergency exits. This should raise alarm bells.

© MATT MUNRO / LONELY PLANET

FOUR OF THE BEST: FREE LAST-MINUTE ACCOMMODATION-BOOKING APPS

Forgot to book your next night on the road? Save money on walk-in rates and avoid the hassle of wandering the streets looking for a room by booking via these handy apps.

★

HOTEL TONIGHT

This app finds users last-minute hotels around the world via '10-second, three-tap bookings'. You can search up to a week ahead, but the best rates appear until noon on the day you plan to stay. The carefully curated categorised hotels show amenities, a user rating and a 'why we like it' tip.

★

JETSETTER

Jetsetter offers discounted luxury hotels, as well as holiday packages. Jetsetter offers bookings year-round alongside its limited-time deals. Each hotel is categorised by the collection it fits into (royal, posh or brilliant). There are filtering options, amenities, as well as tips and reviews.

★

BOOKING.COM

This app is handy for those times you need to widen your search field. The booking.com app will list all available room types, hotel facilities and policies, along with other pertinent information. If you want a number of options that you can filter by price, location, facilities and more, this is for you.

★

HOSTELWORLD

The international hostel and budget guesthouse-booking site is for when you need a budget bed fast. It shows every accommodation provider in the area of your search with availability for your date, information from the host, amenities, room options, ratings, reviews and policies.

EATING AND DRINKING

It's true: mealtimes have the potential to be the loneliest aspects of solo travel. But only if you let them. With a bit of confidence and forward planning, many solo travellers find them perfectly enjoyable, and often a lot of fun.

TABLE FOR ONE: EATING ALONE IN RESTAURANTS

Eating out alone can be a daunting prospect, and can take a while to get used to. If you're a newbie, start small with breakfast or a mid-morning coffee. When you've built up the confidence to go to dinner – which for some reason is often seen as the most taboo mealtime to dine alone – book ahead or avoid the peak rush to ensure you can snag your own table. Booking ahead also tends to save you the confidence-sapping 'just one?' query from staff when you arrive. If you're feeling social, opt to sit at the bar, which tends to provide more opportunities to meet other solos, or at least chat to the bartender.

Check the menu online before you arrive to help prevent panic ordering (which can easily happen when

© PESKYMONKEY / GETTY IMAGES

© RYANJLANE / GETTY IMAGES

© 2014 HWB PHOTOGRAPHY / 500PX

© LAN-OI...

Have a food allergy? Search the web for printable translation cards that you can flash to food vendors who don't speak your language.

you're a little stressed), and bring some props such as your travel journal, mobile (cell) phone or a good book to occupy you while you wait for your meal. Savour the opportunity to people-watch while you eat, and don't be embarrassed if you notice other diners looking at you – humans are a curious lot. Having the right amount of cash on hand to settle your bill can help avoid an awkward wait for change at restaurants in destinations that have a particularly relaxed approach to service (such as Latin America).

EATING IN

Cooking your own meals is a good excuse to stay in when you don't feel like dining out alone, while also saving you money. Many hostels have kitchens for guest use, but don't forget to check it out before you buy supplies (many hostels have a 'free shelf' you might be able to raid, while others may be lacking utensils required to cook certain dishes). Sticking with local produce will invariably be cheaper than trying to replicate your favourite dishes at home; websites like hostelcookers.com are a great source of easy recipes that can be cooked with limited ingredients and utensils.

If you're travelling with food, it's wise to keep it in a secure container to prevent fruit bruising, or jars of food leaking or breaking in your bag – trust us, you do not want a jar of pesto exploding in your backpack! Remember to declare it if you are travelling to a different region or country where the food you're carrying might be banned. Australia, for example, imposes strict fines on people found carrying fresh fruit across certain state lines.

THE SOLO TRAVEL HANDBOOK

HOW TO EAT STREET FOOD WITHOUT GETTING SICK

Street-food dining is a deliciously informal and social affair – there is no need to dress up, and sharing tables with other travellers and locals is typically common. Don't forget to read up on local etiquette – and be savvy about where you eat. Food poisoning can strike anywhere, but you can try to avoid it by following these tips:

★
Busy stalls are a good sign, but check who is in the queue – women and children are less likely to have stomachs as resilient as local taxi drivers'.

★
Note the stallholders' hygiene; if the chef is handling money and food with the same hand (gloved or not), alarm bells should be ringing.

★
Carry your own camping spoon or chopsticks, or wipe down provided cutlery with a baby wipe before using it.

★
Follow local mealtimes – if locals eat dinner at 6pm, the food you buy at 9pm may have been sitting around since it was cooked for the dinner rush.

★
Download or print out a translation card if you suffer from intolerances – use selectwisely.com or allergytranslation.com

★
'Vegetarian' can mean different things. Be specific about exactly which kind of meat you cannot eat.

★
Ensure food that is supposed to be served hot is cooked through.

★
If you can't be sure that meat hasn't been sitting out all day, or has been cooked more than once, don't risk it.

★
Caution is required with ice when outside of major cities where tap water isn't potable. And fruit you can peel yourself is more hygienic.

HITTING THE TOWN AS A SOLO TRAVELLER

Going out at night by yourself while travelling might seem even more daunting than dining alone, but there's no reason why solo travellers should miss out on the fun.

If you like to party, stay at a party hostel, or at least a sociable hostel, where it's typically easy to make friends to go out with. Many hostels refrain from promoting themselves as 'party hostels', but if a hostel advertises drink specials or hosts pub crawls, there's a good chance it's a party hostel.

TOP TIP
Don't allow strangers to buy you a drink, keep your drink in sight, keep your level of intoxication in check, and pre-plan getting back safely.

If you'd rather stay somewhere you can actually get some sleep when you want it, consider bedding down at a quieter hostel or hotel (those with bars or shared common areas are great places to meet people to go out with), and head to the party hostel bar to drink. If that's not your scene, look out for organised nightlife activities offered elsewhere – most cities have food and nightlife tours, meet-ups and night markets, while bars and clubs host special events like trivia and comedy nights that offer a more sociable atmosphere than a typical bar.

Rather roll alone? Aim for a bar where you can get your own table, or at least sit on a barstool, so you aren't left standing around by yourself. Like dining alone, it can be handy to have a prop to keep you occupied, or use as excuse to avoid any unwanted attention. Don't be afraid to strike up conversation with the bartender or other patrons – they might end up being great company. If you have to queue to get in, chat to other people in the line. By the time you reach the front of the line, you may very well have secured your crew for the night.

3 of the best: social-dining apps

Social-dining apps offer great opportunities to get an insight into local life in your travel destination while enjoying a great meal in good company.

EATWITH

EatWith allows you to browse menus from over 650 chefs in more than 200 cities across the globe and book a seat to dine at the chef's own home, typically with the chef's family and other paying guests. Competitor apps BonAppetour and Feastly essentially offer the same service.

VIZEAT

Similarly to EatWith, VizEat allows travellers to book meals cooked by local chefs, but it also offers a range of other bookable culinary experiences in 110 countries, from secret food tours and live music supper clubs, to wine tastings and cooking classes.

WEFIFO

Launched in the UK in 2016 with plans for world domination, WeFiFo (derived from 'We Find Food'), allows home cooks to advertise affordable supper clubs. New hosts begin at 'novice' level charging less than £10 and can work their way up to 'pro' status.

10 TRAVEL HACKS EVERY SOLO TRAVELLER SHOULD KNOW

You're bound to make mistakes on your first solo trip, but you can learn from previous travellers. Monica Stott, founder of thetravelhack.com, has learned a fair bit. Here she shares her top ten hacks.

1 ORDER SPECIAL MEALS ON PLANES

Pre-order a special meal, such as a vegetarian or vegan meal, on flights. Special meals are served first so you'll get your food faster, allowing you to nod off sooner than your seatmates if you're keen to get some rest. The vegan meals are usually healthy, light and delicious, which helps you to avoid that groggy, bloated, post-flight feeling that tends to be a by-product of indulging in a rich plane meal.

2 DRESS UP FOR AIRPORT CHECK-IN

Did you know that solo travellers are more likely to get upgraded on flights? You're also more likely to be upgraded if you look the part, so wear the smartest clothes you're travelling with to the airport (you can always pack a more comfortable set of clothes in your hand luggage to change into after you check in). It's also worth asking at check-in if any upgrade opportunities are available. While it is more difficult to score upgrades these days unless you're a frequent flyer, if you don't ask, you don't get!

3 USE AIRPORT LOUNGES

Airport lounges aren't just for first class passengers; you can often buy yourself into them for a bargain. In the UK, airport lounge passes start from around £25 and include perks such as unlimited snacks and alcohol, wi-fi, magazines, and a quiet and comfortable space to relax before your flight. Using lounges during long layovers offers particularly good value, as it doesn't typically cost much more than you'd spend on food and drink elsewhere in the airport.

© MASKOT / GETTY IMAGES

4 PACK A PORTABLE CHARGER

You'll undoubtedly use your phone a lot while you travel, so pack a portable charger. Make sure to have a way to contact someone in an emergency, and use your phone's GPS for directions. Portable chargers are cheap and lightweight and you'll thank yourself when you're trying to call a taxi at 3am with only 2% battery remaining!

5 DISGUISE YOUR GADGETS

Flashy new devices with crisp, clean cases attract thieves, which is the last thing you want when you're travelling solo. Avoid unwanted attention by making your expensive gadgets look less pricey than they really are – cover your camera in stickers, and buy cheap cases for your smartphone and your tablet and scuff them up.

6 MARK YOUR BAGGAGE AS FRAGILE

Slap a 'fragile' label on your luggage to prevent it from being handled roughly in transit. Adding this label will typically also see your luggage delivered to the baggage carousel - it's often the case that special luggage and equipment is the last to be placed in the aircraft's hold, which means it will be the first to be taken out again.

7 ALWAYS CARRY A BUSINESS CARD FROM YOUR HOTEL

As soon as you arrive at your hotel or hostel, grab a business card from the reception desk with the hotel's address and phone number. If you get lost, you can jump in a taxi and give the card to your driver to ensure you get back to your hotel safely. If a business card isn't available, ask a member of reception staff if they could write down the address in the local language for you. Make sure to then keep the information somewhere handy when you head out to explore.

© HINTERHAUS PRODUCTIONS / GETTY IMAGES

8 TRAVEL WITH AN UNLOCKED MOBILE (CELL) PHONE

If you have a contract phone, ensure it is unlocked before you travel. This means you'll be able to use any SIM card from any mobile network across the world. Pick up a local SIM once you arrive and you'll avoid roaming fees and enjoy cheaper calls and texts – you can find SIM cards at the airport and convenience stores in touristy areas.

© SKA / GETTY IMAGES

9 KEEP YOUR TRAVEL ESSENTIALS IN YOUR SUITCASE AT HOME

Adopt this travel hack if you're a frequent traveller and don't want to forget those all-important essentials. When you return from a trip, leave key items in your suitcase. Items such as your passport, plug adaptors, miniature toiletries and insurance documents can stay in your case because you won't need them at home, and leaving them in your case means you'll never forget to pack them.

10 USE FREE WALKING TOURS TO HELP YOU EASE INTO A NEW CITY

Most cities have free walking tours, and these tend to attract other solo travellers. Solos usually stick together once the tour is over and go for drinks or dinner together, so it's a great opportunity to meet likeminded travellers while simultaneously avoiding the anxiety of dining alone on your first night in town.

THE SOLO TRAVEL HANDBOOK

MEETING PEOPLE

Travelling solo is a great opportunity to learn to love your own company. However, the global travel community is overwhelmingly a friendly one – don't be surprised if you're invited out to dinner by a group of travellers you've just met and don't be afraid to ask to join an activity with other travellers. Locals, too, often make more of an effort to engage solo travellers in conversation. Be receptive to this when it feels safe to do so – you never know what kind of local secrets you may learn.

10 NON-AWKWARD WAYS TO MEET PEOPLE ON THE ROAD

1. JOIN A WALKING TOUR

Not only is this a great (and often free) way to get your bearings in a new city, but the nature of walking tours lend to easy conversation. If the group isn't too large, a good host will ask everyone to say their name and where they're from, which gives you an easy 'in' for striking up conversation with other participants along the way. Stopping for a group meal or drink also presents a great opportunity to socialise.

2. CONNECT ONLINE

There are now loads of apps designed to help travellers connect on the road. Tripr and Backpackr help you meet people ahead of time who will be travelling to the same destinations, EatWith allows you to attend a dinner party hosted by a local chef, and travelstoke can help you find locals and other travellers willing to share advice, meet up or host you.

3. EMBRACE HOSTELS

Look for hostels that have a cool shared space, as these can be great places to meet other travellers over a beer, while cooking meals or simply hanging out. If you're not staying at a hostel, check larger hostel websites for event schedules – many host tours, dinners, pub crawls and other events available to non-guests.

4. RENT A ROOM

Whether it's Couchsurfing or renting a room through Airbnb, stay at a spot where you can engage with your host. Locals who are willing to share their home are usually interested in connecting with their visitors, and these hosts are often a great source of local info.

5. TAKE YOUR MEAL AT THE BAR

Choosing to eat at a restaurant's bar not only allows you to bypass a potentially awkward 'table for one' dining scenario, but it also gives you an opportunity to chat with diners either side of you (who may very well be solo), or with the bartender – staff often make an extra effort to chat to solo patrons.

6. JOIN A LOCAL MEET-UP

The Meetup (meetup.com) community has almost 30 million members in 184 countries, so there's a decent chance there will be an event of interest during your visit. Keen IG'ers can search for local InstaMeets via instagram.com, while travel bloggers can connect at Travel Massive (travelmassive.com) events around the globe.

7. TAKE A COURSE

From cooking courses to tango lessons, classes aimed at visitors offer an opportunity to bond with other travellers over a shared interest, not to mention the experience of trying to master it.

8. SIGN UP FOR GROUP TOURS

From day trips to multi-day adventures, small-group tours offer travel experiences that you aren't able to access as an independent traveller, as well as an opportunity to form friendships – that can be lifelong – with the people you share the journey with. Choose an active tour, as you are not likely to meet anyone other than your seatmate on a standard city bus tour.

9. OFFER TO TAKE PHOTOS

If you spot another tourist struggling to take a selfie, or perhaps you see them taking a photo of a scene that would look great with them in it, offer to take a shot for them. They may offer to take one for you, too, providing a natural icebreaker for asking where they are from, and what brings them to the destination.

10. VOLUNTEER YOUR TIME

Check hostel noticeboards and meetup. com for community projects you may be able to get involved in for an afternoon or longer – this offers an opportunity to bond with other travellers over the warm fuzzy feeling of giving back.

WORKING

Keen to supplement your travel savings to help keep you on the road for longer? Putting yourself to work while travelling also offers the chance to forge more meaningful friendships, gain a deeper understanding of local culture, learn new skills and explore your host destination in more depth than you would if you were simply passing through as a regular traveller. Unless you work remotely, working visas are typically a legal requirement for paying jobs. However, there are plenty of other ways to make – or at least save – money by trading your time and skills.

10 GREAT WORK OPPORTUNITIES FOR TRAVELLERS

1. WORK AT A HOSTEL

One of the easiest and most popular ways for travellers to work on the road without a work permit, working at a hostel can involve anything from bartending and cleaning dorms, to serving food and manning the front desk (whether you have experience or not). This work – typically four to six hours a day, five to six days per week – is usually offered in exchange for free board and meals, for stints of around one month.

2. TEACH ENGLISH

With a Teachers of English to Speakers of Other Languages (TESOL), Teaching English as a Foreign Language (TEFL) or similar qualification, there is decent money to be made in teaching English overseas, with countries including China, Japan, Korea, Taiwan and the Middle East offering among the highest salaries (up to around US$5000 per month in Korea, for example). Teaching a language, however, generally commands a commitment of at least several months.

3. USE YOUR SKILLS

Can you teach yoga or build websites? Many travellers use their skills in return for everything from hostel accommodation to tours – and even cash. The hostel, tour operator or other local business might not even know it needs you until you approach it with your pitch, so don't be afraid to test it out.

4. WORK ONLINE

If you dream of spending your life on the road, working online is typically the key to maintaining this lifestyle. Check out sites like problogger.com, freelancer.com and upwork.com for listings of remote work gigs from copywriting and graphic design, to app development and accounting. Rates vary, but there is no lack of options.

5. TRAVEL PHOTOGRAPHY AND WRITING

Established writers and photographers will find this avenue more lucrative, but there are plenty of avenues for newbies to build their profile and make a bit of money in the process. Travel website matadornetwork.com pays around US$40 for an 800- to 1000-word travel article, while bootsnall.com pays US$50 for a 1200- to 2000-word story; visit the respective websites for guidelines. There are also a growing number of opportunities for selling your travel photos. Among the more profitable (with opportunities to earn more than US$100 per photo) include shutterstock.com, 500px.com and istockphoto.com.

6. WORKING FOR BOARD

Organisations such as workaway.info and wwoofinternational.org are just two of a handful that list opportunities to perform a number of odd jobs around family homes, businesses and farms in return for accommodation and food. Generally speaking, working five hours per day, five days per week, in return for accommodation (usually shared) and two to three meals per day, is a fair deal. Jobs can range from cleaning holiday huts and maintaining hiking trails, to feeding horses and picking carrots. Hosts typically require a minimum one-month commitment, but shorter placements are available.

7. SEASONAL WORK

Fruit picking is especially popular in Australia, where a second working holiday visa can be secured by travellers who commit to 88 days of paid work in a designated regional location (check fruitpickingjobs.com.au for listings). Other popular seasonal jobs include working at a summer camp in the US, or at a ski resort in a country with an established international seasonal worker community such as Australia, Austria, France, New Zealand and the US. Valid working permits are typically required.

8. AU PAIR

Love kids and have some childcare experience? While most au pair opportunities require at least a six-month commitment, some families only require a nanny for holiday periods that can be as short as several weeks. Check listings on au pair job sites such as aupair.com, aupairworld.com and findaupair.com.

9. BE A FILM EXTRA

If you're travelling in India, strolling around the Colaba area of Mumbai might very well see you scouted for a part in a Bollywood film – Colaba Causeway (try the Leopold Cafe) and the Gateway of India are particularly popular scouting hot spots. Don't expect to earn more than about 500Rp (US$7.50) for a day's work, but most would argue the novelty factor is worth it.

10. WORK AT A FESTIVAL

If you're planning to be travelling in a destination hosting a festival, consider joining its volunteer force. In return for a festival ticket (and sometimes also meals), you will typically be required to perform several shifts ranging from scanning tickets to pouring beers. Check individual festival websites for opportunities, or sign up with oxfam.org.uk/stewarding in the UK, and workexchangeteam.com in the US, which organise volunteers for a number of festivals in each country.

WORKING FOR FREE

Volunteering your precious holiday time for a good cause is a noble gesture, and there are thousands of organisations out there willing to sign you up for projects ranging from building schools to monitoring turtle nests. Be sure to research opportunities thoroughly before signing on to ensure your contribution will be both beneficial to the cause as well as meaningful for you. See p95 for more info on responsible volunteering.

TOP TIP

'If your main goal of working for board is to save money to keep you on the road for longer, don't forget to factor in the costs involved in getting yourself to the host location. I did a great project on a little island in British Columbia, Canada, where I didn't spend a cent for three weeks, but the transport I needed to take to get there, including ferries and land transfers, took a chunk out of my savings.' SIMON SOUTHEY, WORKAWAY VETERAN

DOCUMENTING YOUR TRIP

Whether you're interested in documenting your travel experience for your own eyes, or you dream of leveraging your content into a bona-fide career, it pays to have a strategy.

THE CAMERA CONUNDRUM

There's no denying it: travelling with bulky and/or expensive camera gear will increase your vulnerability on any trip, let alone a solo adventure. So depending where you're headed, you might have to make a compromise. If you aren't looking to use your images professionally, do you really need to bring your DSLR and bulky zoom lens? If high-quality photography is important to you, are you prepared to take extra security measures to ensure the protection of your gear?

'If you're looking to travel light and still take great photos, I would definitely recommend taking a mirrorless camera (such as a cross between a DLSR and a point-and-shoot) and selecting one great variable lens to bring with you,' says photographer Lauren Bath, one of the world's first professional Instagrammers. 'The Olympus OM D E M1 Mark II I am using at the moment has great image stabilisation, which gives me the flexibility to leave my tripod at home as well if I want to travel even lighter.'

Of course, the humble smartphone cannot be dismissed as a photography tool. If you don't need high-resolution images to sell or print out, a smartphone with a decent camera (generally speaking, the newer the phone, the better the camera) might be the best option for you. For video and adventure photography, a GoPro camera (gopro.com) with a waterproof housing can also come in handy.

HOW TO TAKE GREAT PHOTOS

'I look at taking pictures like building blocks,' says Bath. 'Start with a photogenic subject and then add amazing light (sunrise and sunset, known as the 'golden hour' is best), double-check your composition (see box), and then consider putting yourself into the scene for scale. There is always something you can do to turn a good photo into a great photo.'

'Just by understanding your camera settings and shooting at golden hour you will instantly improve your snaps,' Bath adds. 'Use that as a starting point and then build from there.'

5 techniques to remember when composing a photo

1. RULE OF THIRDS
Divide the frame into a nine-rectangle grid (some cameras have a grid mode) and ensure the important elements of the picture straddle at least two lines. You can better the composition by framing the subject off-centre.

2. HORIZON LINE
Check the horizon line is straight. This can be fixed up with photo editing software.

3. LEADING LINES
Ensure there are lines leading towards the focus. Use anything from pathways and walls, to driftwood or clouds.

4. NEGATIVE SPACE
Leaving lots of empty space around your subject creates minimalism that helps the viewer focus on the subject.

5. DYNAMIC TENSION
Use movement to draw the eye in contrasting directions. Lines moving away from each other or mirrored body language.

© KOLBEIN SVENSSON / 500PX

5 steps to getting a stranger to take a great photo of you

1. CHOOSE THE RIGHT PERSON

Look for someone who doesn't seem in a rush. Ideally this person will be carrying a quality camera.

2. ASK NICELY

Remember to thank them and ask if they would like you to return the favour.

3. BRIEF THE STRANGER AS BEST YOU CAN

Let them know if you would prefer the shot in portrait or landscape style, and whether you'd like them to zoom in or not.

4. ADJUST YOUR CAMERA SETTINGS BEFORE YOU HAND OVER YOUR CAMERA

Set up the camera on a tripod and ask the stranger to press the shutter button.

5. USE THE HIGH-SPEED BLAST SETTING

Ask the stranger to hold down the shutter while you try a few poses.

THE THING ABOUT SELFIES

The selfie stick has revolutionised self-portrait-taking for solo travellers. But if you are after a quality portrait shot in a photogenic location, selfie sticks don't beat a tripod, says Bath. 'A selfie stick will get you selfies, but a tripod will get you beautiful landscape images with yourself in the frame,' she says.

If you do plan to travel with a selfie stick, remember to use it responsibly, being mindful of other travellers when you wave your selfie stick around trying to find the best angle. It's worth reading up on international selfie stick laws, too, as the sticks are now banned in popular tourist hot spots and galleries, museums and music festivals worldwide.

HOW TO TAKE THE PERFECT SELFIE

Remember the three key points of this selfie mantra and you'll take perfect self-portraits every time.

1.
ENVIRONMENT

Ensure the background and lighting is just right before you strike your pose.

2.
POSING

Know your best angle and learn which selfie smile works for you, from the 'tongue touch' (placing your tongue on the roof of your mouth and smiling without showing your teeth) to the 'close and open' (close and then slowly open your eyes, and draw up the corners of your mouth to a smile). Avoid the 'duck face' pout.

3.
EDITING

Learn how to use Instagram filters ('clarendon' is the most popular Instagram filter) and don't forget to crop your shot nicely before posting it.

SOCIAL MEDIA SMARTS FOR SOLO TRAVELLERS

An ever-expanding realm of social media platforms – from Facebook to Snapchat, Instagram to Twitter – has made it much easier to stay in touch with friends and loved ones while you're on the road, but not all travellers are aware of the safest ways to use them. Consider the following before making your next post, especially if you're travelling alone.

★

Posting status updates while you are on holiday sends a clear message to your 'friends' (and strangers, depending on the platform and your privacy settings) that you are not at home. This potentially makes you susceptible to thieves.

★

Tagging travel buddies in your photos while you are still on holiday also compromises their privacy – they may not want the internet to know where they are.

★

Posting photos while you are travelling with the geotag function enabled makes your precise location available to a wide range of people, which can compromise your safety.

★

Posting upcoming travel plans also lets your followers know where you are headed, which may also risk your security.

For more advice on staying safe while travelling solo, flip to p86.

THE KEY TO A KILLER INSTAGRAM FEED

Travel Instagramming has turned into a lucrative career for some travellers who, thanks to their sizeable followings, are able to leverage big pay checks from business partners. Whether you harbour dreams of being Insta-famous or would simply like to grow your following, Bath says diversity and consistency of your posts is key.

'If the photographer is doing the same thing all the time I get bored,' says Bath. 'I also love to see new posts going up regularly, at least one a day.'

You can also improve your Instagram account by having a good bio, funny or informative captions and high-quality images.

SHOULD YOU KEEP A JOURNAL?

Keeping a traditional travel diary might sound old school, but the benefits are aplenty. Not only does journalising keep you occupied while you're waiting to check in for a flight, or when you're dining alone, but your notes can serve as a fantastic resource down the track when a friend asks for a hotel recommendation in Barcelona, or where they can find those life-changing empanadas in Mexico City you told them about. If you've written it down, you can always quick-reference your journal if you forget. From a practical point of view, a journal is also a great place to keep note of your expenses if you're not a fan of mobile apps designed for this purpose (p55).

TOP TIP

'I love using the Paper by FiftyThree app to make quick sketches on my iPhone or iPad with a digital pencil when I'm travelling without a sketchbook. The app makes it really easy to capture notes, photos and sketches, and organise them for easy reference down the track.' EMMA TAMAOKI, ILLUSTRATOR AND GRAPHIC DESIGNER

SO, YOU WANT TO BE A TRAVEL BLOGGER?

Starting a travel blog is a great way to share your travel escapades with friends and family, and it is free and easy to create a simple blog on a number of platforms such as tumblr.com, wordpress.com and blogger.com. Becoming a professional travel blogger, however, is a whole different ballgame.

To get started, you'll need to choose a blogging platform that offers more flexibility than free blogging platforms and purchase a domain name and a website-hosting plan. You will also need to invest in templates and plug-ins to make your blog more attractive and user-friendly, or recruit a website developer. And then there's the content to create, and a readership to build to give you leverage for securing advertisers, brand partnerships and other opportunities. Success won't come overnight, but if you have the passion, the commitment and the patience, anything is possible. To learn more tricks of the travel blogging trade, visit travelblogsuccess.com.

STAYING CONNECTED

As much as the idea of unplugging on holiday might tickle your wanderlust receptors, taking the time to keep in regular contact with loved ones back home is as important for maintaining your personal relationships as it is for your safety.

Thanks to modern technology, staying in touch is a whole lot easier than it once used to be. But we're not just talking about social media platforms and the plethora of free calling and texting apps. Beyond the usual suspects, there are a growing number of ways to make staying connected more fun.

TOP TIP

'When I need a wi-fi connection and don't want to use my data roaming, I use the Wi-Fi Finder app. Simply choose your location and the app displays local wi-fi connections on a map, along with pertinent info including connection status (free or private), connection speed, connection privacy level and user ratings.'
ISABEL ALBISTON, LONELY PLANET WRITER

© HENN PHOTOGRAPHY / GETTY IMAGES

4 QUIRKY APPS FOR STAYING CONNECTED ON THE ROAD

1. LIVETREKKER

Is there someone at home who would kill to join you on your Himalayan hike? Now they can, thanks to this app that allows you to create a digital journal of your journey on an interactive map. You can add pictures, text, audio and video along the way, creating a multimedia travel diary you can share with whomever you like, whenever you like.

2. TOUCHNOTE

This fun app allows you to send photos from your travels as physical postcards. Once you have selected your photo and message, Touchnote will print and post the cards for you – typically for a lower cost than you would pay for postage from your current travel destination.

3. FLIPAGRAM

If you're keen to arrange your holiday snaps into some sort of narrative – or you just want to show off your craft cocktail from multiple angles – this is an essential download. All you have to do is select your favourite photos, sequence them, and choose a track from your iTunes (or from an online database) to use as the soundtrack, and the lot will be 'flipped' into a slideshow that you can post away on Facebook.

4. TRIPCAST

Perfect for travellers who want to share every moment of their journey with loved ones at home, Tripcast allows you to create a photo album and invite friends and family to follow along. They'll then be able to see every single photo that you post in real time, together with a location tag, and be able to 'like' and comment on images.

11 WAYS TO OVERCOME LONELINESS WHILE TRAVELLING SOLO

No matter how many amazing experiences you enjoy, the journey can get a little lonely. Here are some tricks to help.

2) TREAT YOURSELF

Think about what you love doing by yourself that you rarely find the time to do at home. Travelling for an extended period of time almost always means travelling on a budget but, once in while, reward yourself by staying at a nice hotel after camping for two weeks straight, or booking yourself into a spa after a long bus journey. Enjoy the moment and carry on with your trip feeling refreshed and re-energised.

3) GO EXPLORE

When you're feeling down, staying curled up in bed all day isn't going to help. Take advantage of being in a new destination and go for a walk; finding your way around will help to take your mind off feeling lonely. If the sun is out, you'll get a vitamin D boost to help cheer you up, too.

1) MAKE A LIST

Refocus your energy on the task at hand. Why are you on this trip? What do you want to accomplish? Trade loneliness for ambition and physically write out a plan of action. Have you always wanted to learn to scuba dive, speak Spanish or learn how to tango? Now is the time to tick it off your list.

7) CONNECT WITH YOUR LOVED ONES

Nothing quite snaps you out of feeling sorry for yourself than touching base with people back home who would kill to be in your travel shoes. Sometimes just hearing a familiar voice is enough to cheer you up.

8) JOIN A GROUP TOUR

Even if you aren't particularly looking to make new friends, just being in the company of others is a good way to stem loneliness. Try to book activities through a hostel, which usually means you'll be joined by other solo travellers rather than couples and families. After a day of socialising, you may even find yourself looking forward to some alone time when the tour ends.

4) FIND A TRAVEL COMPANION

Who's to say your solo trip can't involve buddying up with other travellers along the way? Hooking up with another solo traveller or a group can often enrich your trip, opening you up to travel experiences you might not have known about or considered doing alone. See p66 for top tips on how to meet people on the road.

5) TALK TO LOCALS

Break out of your shell by making an effort to converse with locals. Question your hotel staff for their favourite places to eat, and take the time to ask shopkeepers how their day is going – you may be pleasantly surprised where these conversations lead.

6) STAY AT HOSTELS

It is difficult to feel lonely at a hostel, in which you typically can't escape the company of others. Make an effort to get to know your dorm-mates, and sign up for hostel-run social activities like pub crawls and communal meals.

9) SWEAT IT OUT

There's nothing like an exercise-triggered endorphin rush to make you feel good about yourself. Withdrawing from exercise has been linked to depression, so if you've let your regular exercise routine slip during your travels, this might explain why you are feeling a little down. If you aren't able to go for a run or hit the gym, do some yoga or squats and push-ups in your room, or sign up for an active day tour.

10) USE COUCHSURFING

If you're travelling in a destination where social opportunities are slim, consider using Couchsurfing (couchsurfing.com). This online community offers travellers free accommodation in their homes. Often your host will also show you around the city, have a meal with you or simply just hang out with you.

11) SMILE

It might sound simple, but it's the truth – smile and people will be more receptive to you. If you appear sullen and have a negative attitude, people will subconsciously avoid talking to you.

HEALTH AND FITNESS

With travel often providing ample opportunities for poolside lazing and gorging on gourmet buffet meals, staying fit and healthy on the road isn't always easy. Keeping your health in check, however, will not only help you stay more alert and aware of your personal safety (p91), but it will also help you better manage those times when you do fall ill on the road.

A BALANCING ACT

There's nothing wrong with a little indulgence on holiday, but abandoning your usual routine can leave you feeling lethargic, irritable and easy to tire – none of which are ideal while travelling. If you aren't eating more than usual on the road, chances are you'll be drinking more, so try to balance it with exercise. Make use of the hotel gym or, if there isn't one, use your own body as a gym by doing some sit-ups, squats or yoga in your room, in a park or on the beach. If you're not keen to work out, step up your incidental exercise: take the stairs instead of the elevator, or sign up for activities like kayaking, hiking or even just walking tours.

TOP TIP

'I never travel anywhere without my trainers. If you have comfy shoes, you can skip taxis and explore on foot. Not only does this give you a chance to really immerse yourself in the destination, you'll also be exercising and burning calories without even noticing. To make the walk challenging, pack heavier items in your day pack – this burns more calories as you have to work harder to carry the extra weight.'
SARAH O'FARRELL, TRAVEL AND FITNESS BLOGGER, FITTRAVELS.COM

BELOW Doing the necessary training for an active holiday will decrease your injury risk and boost the fun factor.

SEXUAL HEALTH

Solo travel brings a sense of freedom that might very well make you more likely to tumble into bed with another traveller (or a local) than you would at home. Practising safe sex on the road might not seem much different to practising it at home, but before you indulge in a holiday fling, it's important to consider a few things. Firstly, make sure you have brought contraception from home.

'Contraception sold in some countries can be inferior to the contraceptives available at home,' says travel doctor Dr Deborah 'Deb' Mills, author of travel health bible *Travelling Well.* 'Condoms, for example, can be smaller in regions like Asia than in Western countries, making them more susceptible to breaking.'

If the condom breaks during sex in a country where the morning-after pill isn't available or easily accessible, you may have to cut your trip short to head home if you are not willing to risk the chance that you may be pregnant.

Travel has also been linked to an increased chance of contracting an STI – gonorrhoea, chlamydia, and hepatitis B and C are typically the most common infections, but there are plenty of other nasties out there that might not only ruin your trip, but affect you for the rest of your life if you don't protect yourself. Hepatitis C, for example (which is also commonly transmitted by tattoo needles) can be managed, but the disease is currently incurable.

© JORDAN SIEMENS / GETTY IMAGES

BUYING (AND TRAVELLING WITH) MEDICATION ON THE ROAD

Chances are there'll be something you forgot to pack, or an item you need to restock, that will see you needing to visit a local pharmacy. Just remember, says Dr Deb, not to treat it like a trip to your pharmacy at home.

'In some countries, typically developing countries, what it says on the packet might not be what's inside the packet,' says Dr Deb, who advises purchasing medication abroad only when absolutely necessary. Remember to check expiry dates, as expired drugs can be ineffective or have an adverse reaction.

'When travelling with medication, remember to bring a letter from your doctor that authorises you to be carrying it,' says Dr Deb, who also advises reading up on local laws to ensure it is legal to carry your drugs into your destination. Codeine, for example, is restricted in the UAE and you cannot bring it into the country without presenting your prescription.

MEDICAL EMERGENCY?

With any luck, you won't need to use the emergency hotline for your travel insurance provider. But in the event you need assistance, don't hesitate to call, says Dr Deb. 'Travellers forget that their travel insurance provider sort of works like a concierge service for medical advice. If you got bitten by an animal and think you may need a rabies vaccine, for example, call your provider and they should be able to tell you the best place to go locally to get treated.'

If you do need to take yourself to hospital, be sure to let your accommodation know where you are going, and call someone at home so they know how to check up on you.

5 TIPS FOR MAINTAINING GOOD HYGIENE ON THE ROAD

+1. Wash your hands as often as possible, and keep a bottle of hand sanitiser in your day pack for situations when soap and water is not available.

+2. If it's not safe to drink the tap water in the destination, you shouldn't be washing your toothbrush under it, either.

+3. Wear flip-flops in communal showers. Aside from the risk of contracting fungal infections like tinea, there is a risk of contracting other icky pathogens if you step into the shower with an open wound on your foot.

+4. Opt for disposable bamboo chopsticks, or use your own camping spoon, if you're dubious about the cleanliness of cutlery provided.

+5. Drink lots of water to stay hydrated and keep your urinary tract healthy – don't avoid water just because you're scared you might not find a toilet.

SAFETY

Going solo requires special attention to travel safety. That's not to say that solo travel is unsafe – in fact, it can often be safer than travelling with a partner or in a group, which entices travellers to let their guard down. But when you don't have a travel buddy to watch your back – or bail you out in an emergency – it really pays to know the safety risks in your destination to better help you avoid them.

TOP 20 WAYS TO STAY SAFE ON THE ROAD

1 Ensure you have emailed your travel documents (including copies of your bankcards) to yourself, and to a friend or family member at home, so you can easily access copies if needed.

2 Pack light so that you can manage your luggage yourself with ease, and be wary of people who offer to help you with your bags – most people genuinely want to help you, but some don't.

3 Arrange regular check-ins with someone at home so they know where you are, and in what circumstances an alarm should be raised.

4 Plan to arrive in a new destination during daylight hours so you don't have to find your way to your accommodation in the dark. If that's not possible, arrange a transfer to your accommodation, or take a taxi.

5 Ask staff at your accommodation to mark safe and unsafe areas on a destination map for you, as they are likely to have the most up-to-date information on this subject.

6 Lock important items in your room safe or locker, and keep your day-to-day valuables close to you at all times – but never in your back pocket, or at the top of your day pack.

7 When it's not possible to lock your valuables away, conceal them in your luggage – tampon boxes or condom packets make good places to stash cash and credit cards.

8 Carry the business card of your accommodation with you when you venture out; it should list the address in the local language.

9 Stay alert at all times. Your level of alertness decreases with each alcoholic drink. If you must drink, never let a stranger buy for you, and don't let your drink out of your sight.

10 Ensure you have emailed your travel documents (including copies of your bankcards) to yourself, and to a friend or family member at home, so you can easily access copies if needed.

11 Don't let on to strangers where you're staying. Your accommodation should be your safe haven.

12 Walk with confidence everywhere – like you absolutely know where you are going and what you're doing.

13 Be polite to strangers, but don't let being polite compromise your safety – never be afraid to say no.

14 Don't attract attention to yourself by wearing expensive jewellery or flashing your new camera around. On the other end of the spectrum, nothing screams 'naïve tourist' like hippie pants. Try to dress like locals (or local expats) to help you blend in.

15 Understand the destination's transit system (how safe it is, what fares cost, how tickets work and what the main routes are) before you use it.

16 If you are heading out at night, return to your accommodation by taxi – don't risk walking, or taking public transport, if there are safety risks involved.

17 Save numbers including where you're staying, your travel insurance provider, your government's local consulate office and the country's main emergency number.

18 If you are planning to have sex with someone you don't know very well, tell someone you trust where you are going. Tell your partner that you are doing so to increase your safety.

19 Take out small amounts of cash frequently rather than carrying large amounts of money on you, and keep an emergency stash hidden on your body.

20 The attention might be flattering, but be wary of people or groups of people who try to befriend you; it can be more difficult to spot a con artist in a foreign country.

THE SOLO TRAVEL HANDBOOK

WOMEN'S SAFETY

It is an unfortunate reality that female solo travellers typically attract more unwanted attention overseas than solo male travellers. Hence, there are additional precautions women should consider taking on the road.

★

Be aware of local customs. In some countries and regions, a woman's social behaviour and dress can elicit unwanted advances from local men.

★

Never admit that you are travelling alone. Pretending that you are on your way to meet your boyfriend or husband can be a handy trick for getting rid of unwanted attention.

★

Consider wearing a wedding ring (and check in advance to find out which finger of which hand it should be worn on in your destination). Some countries, including the US, recommend solo women wear a wedding ring when travelling to the Middle East.

★

Women-only dorms, and women-only transport carriages, are designed to offer women an added degree of security should you wish to take up these opportunities.

💡 TOP TIP

'You might think taking a tour is beneath you, but I'll let you in on a secret: sometimes travelling with a group can be the safest way to explore a particular destination, especially if you're on your own. If you want to see more, use the tour to get you started and then build in some extra time at the end of the tour to explore alone. In a handful of countries like Iran and Bhutan, travelling as part of a group is a visa requirement for most nationalities, anyway. Do your research and choose small groups of like-minded travellers.' TASMIN WABY, LONELY PLANET DESTINATION EDITOR

★

Keep your wits about you when using free accommodation services like Couchsurfing; there have been reports of assaults on women.

★

Consider travelling with personal safety devices such as a whistle, capsicum spray or a doorstop alarm. Be aware that capsicum spray usually can't be carried in your cabin baggage. It may also be illegal in some countries.

★

Consider installing an alarm or other personal safety apps on your mobile (cell) phone (see p90).

★

Be aware of your rights if you are the victim of an assault. In some countries, including the UAE, rape is considered akin to having sex out of wedlock, which is illegal and could see you thrown in jail for the simple act of reporting the offence.

5 FREE APPS FOR STAYING SAFE

Your mobile (cell) phone can be your most valuable safety tool when travelling. Ensure your data plan can be used abroad, or purchase a local SIM with a decent data plan for the extra degree of safety it provides in allowing you to use many personal safety apps.

1. BSAFE

This clever app allows you to create a 'social safety network' of contacts that will be notified in case of an emergency or in situations where the user feels unsafe, and hits the panic button.

2. CITYMAPPER

Simply punch in your desired destination in one of 39 cities in 21 countries, and this app will show you how to get there via all methods of local transport.

3. COMPANION

For extra safety when walking around at night or in sketchy neighbourhoods, this app texts a link to a live map of your walk to your pre-selected 'companions'. If there is a problem the app will ask you if you are OK or if you want to call the police. If you don't respond within 15 seconds, the app will notify your companions.

4. MAPS.ME

This app allows you to download maps to use offline anywhere in the world.

5. BUGLE

This app is designed primarily for people who don't want to take their phone with them when they're out. Users set the time limit and their emergency contacts in their phone are alerted by email and text if they don't check in within the limit.

5 COMMON TRAVEL SCAMS TO LOOK OUT FOR WHILE TRAVELLING – SOLO OR NOT

'THE METER IS BROKEN'

Demand the driver use the meter or find another taxi. If that's not possible, know what the standard rate is and demand it. It's also useful to know how much time it should take to get to your destination, and which direction you should be travelling in.

'THERE'S S* ON YOUR SHOE'**

A local taps you on the shoulder to tell you that a bird has done the deed on your shoe. As you look down, the 'helpful' stranger's accomplice swipes your wallet and runs away. Don't be another statistic and keep walking if you see this coming.

'YOU'RE BEAUTIFUL'

A lothario charms the socks off you and invites you to a fancy dinner. He realises he has 'forgotten' his wallet, and you end up paying. You invite him back to your room and in the morning, he is gone, along with your valuables. Protect yourself by avoiding a con artist.

'I'LL JUST WRAP THAT FOR YOU'

In what's known as a substitution scam, the vendor switches the item you purchased with a fake or lower quality item. To avoid being duped, never let purchases out of your sight. The same goes for credit cards!

'YOUR HOTEL IS CLOSED, BUT I CAN TAKE YOU SOMEWHERE BETTER'

A local (usually a taxi driver) tells you the hotel you have booked (or the attraction you want to see) is closed, but he can take you somewhere better. So you agree, and the driver makes a juicy commission for taking you to his mate's guesthouse or store. You may be duped into buying dodgy gems or other products.

RESPONSIBLE SOLO TRAVEL

Responsible tourism is all about leaving a positive impact on both the environment and the people who live in the places we choose to visit. Don't let this concept daunt you – responsible travel is not about limiting ways in which you can explore the world, but opening up more layers of the planet's amazing potential to surprise and captivate you. Travelling responsibly needn't have to cost more, nor should it suck the fun out of your adventure. And all it takes to nail it is a little bit of research...

10 GREAT WAYS TO BE A MORE RESPONSIBLE TRAVELLER

1 Educate yourself about your destination and its people so you can speak, behave and dress appropriately. This typically leads to more meaningful cultural experiences.

2 Choose small group tour operators, which tend to have a lower environmental impact. Membership of an organisation like The International Ecotourism Society (ecotourism.org) is a good sign that the operator tries to conduct itself in a responsible manner.

3 Decant biodegradable toiletries into bottles you can reuse on future trips instead of buying travel-size versions of your favourite products, which can typically end up in landfill.

4 Don't believe what it says on the tin when it comes to 'eco' tours and accommodation. Ask operators to spell out their eco-friendly initiatives. Do they employ local staff and pay fair wages? Do they have environmental guidelines?

5 Resist the temptation to be wasteful just because you're on holiday. Turn off the lights, the TV and the air-con in your hotel room when you're not using them, and avoid single-use plastic, such as hotel toiletries and cocktail straws.

6 Avoid tours that promise hands-on interactions with captive wild animals. This supports an industry that illegally captures, transports and abuses millions of animals each year.

7 Do not give pens, sweets or other gifts to local children – it fosters a begging economy. If you wish to donate, contact a local school or organisation that can ensure appropriate gifts are distributed appropriately.

8 Opt for locally made, sustainably produced souvenirs, which helps to preserve local culture. Avoid anything made from endangered plants/ animals, unsustainable hardwoods or ancient artefacts.

9 Try to eat local, in-season produce in destinations you visit. Imagine the carbon miles accrued by a hunk of New Zealand steak served in London!

10 Set a good example to other travellers. If you see other travellers acting irresponsibly, ask them to stop – they may not even know what they are doing is wrong.

TOP TIP

'I never travel without a durable BPA-free water bottle, a canvas carry bag and even a reusable drinking straw for those sunset cocktail moments on the road – metal straws are more widely available these days and make a great gift for travellers. By limiting the amount of plastic you use on holiday, you can have a huge impact – over 500 million plastic straws are used in the US each day alone, with devastating environmental consequences.' SARAH REID, TRAVEL WRITER

SO, YOU WANT TO VOLUNTEER?

Signing up for a volunteer project abroad is a great way to ease into solo travel, but it's crucial to do your research. Sadly, many volunteer organisations do not act in the best interests of travellers, nor the communities, children or wildlife they work with. Wannabe volunteers should be particularly cautious of volunteering opportunities with children in the developing world, says James Sutherland, international communications coordinator of Friends-International, which runs child-protection initiative ChildSafe (thinkchildsafe.org).

'If you are unqualified in childcare and lack other skills (such as medical training) that are not available locally, would you be able to do this work in your own country? The answer is "no",' says Sutherland. 'However well-meaning your intentions, you actually run the real risk of causing further harm to the children.'

Orphanage visits are also discouraged by child-protection experts. 'Many orphanages are run as businesses that have little or no child protection policies or procedures in place,' says Sutherland. 'Numerous clinical studies have also highlighted that a revolving door of visitors to institutionalised children is harmful to the children's long-term emotional and psychological development.'

That's not to say you can't help. 'If you do have transferable skills, consider spending your time transferring them to local staff,' says Sutherland. 'This will have a long-term and sustainable positive impact long after you've headed home.'

Sutherland also suggests directing your support to local organisations that run initiatives helping children and their families. This could be community projects making and selling souvenirs, social businesses or restaurants that train local youth.

There are some fantastic opportunities out there, but you should be sceptical about opportunities that allow unskilled travellers to interact with captive wildlife. Visit responsibletravel.com for an excellent range of volunteer travel opportunities with wildlife and communities.

TOP TIP

'After leaving my dream job to travel for far longer than I initially anticipated, I was nervous about my first big job interview, four years after leaving the permanent workforce. Concerned that my interviewer may interpret my extended travels as a reluctance to be tied down, I sold myself as a candidate who was refreshed, inspired and ready to sit still and apply my new-found skills to the position. Fortunately, it worked.'

SARAH REID, TRAVEL WRITER

PLANNING FOR YOUR RETURN

As fun as it is to indulge the fantasy of travelling forever, if you're not one of the lucky few who are able to turn that dream into a reality, you will have to return to the real world at some point. Knowing what to expect when you come home can make all the difference in ensuring a smooth transition.

BEATING THE POST-TRAVEL BLUES

Returning home from a trip – especially a long one – can be a shock to the system. This shock can manifest in feelings of sadness ranging from disappointment that you no longer get to wake up to the sound of the ocean lapping at the door of your thatched bungalow, to becoming frustrated and miserable that your home life pales in comparison to the freedom you experienced on the road. So how do you manage it? Travel psychologists say incorporating the best bits of your travels into your life back home – from reliving some of your trip's best meals by cooking them for your family, to organising a travel-themed party with friends – can help. Or, you know, you could cheer yourself up by refocusing some of your energies into planning your next trip...

MANAGING FRIENDSPECTATIONS

Stepping off the plane after a trip, you'll no doubt be eager to share your travel stories with your mates and find out what they've been up to while you were away. But when you meet face-to-face, you may find that you don't have so much in common with some of them any more. The realisation that you have drifted apart can be devastating, but the truth is that friends move in and out of your life regardless of whether you travel or not – and, while losing a friend can come as a tough blow during the emotionally testing period after returning from a trip, being prepared for the possibility that some friendships might not withstand the test of time (and, in this case, distance) will help to soften the blow. On the upside, travelling can help to clarify which friendships in your life are truly meaningful and those that only felt skin-deep, thus allowing you to focus your energies on the relationships that matter.

Even good friends, however, can only sit through so many iterations of your life-changing trek in Peru. Give them a break by reaching out to people who have shared the same experiences the next time you feel an urge to reminisce, as they'll be much more eager to relive the adventure with you.

GOING BACK TO WORK

If you left your job to travel – or perhaps you went travelling after studying and have yet to enter the professional workforce – it pays to know how to use your trip to your advantage when you begin your job hunt. Rather than letting your time out of the workforce be a source of anxiety, see it as an opportunity.

'More and more, companies are looking for people who can demonstrate that they are "global citizens,"' says Rosemary Lemon, Group Head of Reward at global recruitment company Hays, who suggests highlighting your travels as a major part of your development. Perhaps you learnt a language, participated in a volunteer project, or fine-tuned your photography skills? Talk up how travelling solo around Eastern Europe fine-tuned your problem-solving ability, or how sticking to a $20/day budget in India for two months refined your budgeting skills. As your trip is coming to an end, carve out some time to tidy up and send out your CV to several recruiters before you return home to give you a head-start on securing interviews.

INSPIRATION:

10 GREAT TRIPS FOR SOLO TRAVELLERS

TOP TIP

Consider taking preventative medication to thwart altitude sickness, which is a particular risk in Bolivia (especially if you fly into La Paz, which sits above 4000m).

Practicalities

✈ Buenos Aires, Argentina; Rio de Janeiro, Brazil; Cartagena, Colombia; Lima, Peru.

LGBT-friendly ★★★☆☆

💼 Invest in a pair of sturdy but breathable walking shoes, rather than heavy leather hiking boots, if you'll be travelling for a while. These will be suitable for most popular treks, and won't weigh you down.

📅 It is always a good time to be somewhere in South America. Hit Brazil's beaches and visit Patagonia in November to March. The calmest seas are December to June for cruising Ecuador's Galápagos islands.

$ / $ ▢ ▢ ▢

○ Adventure
○ Culture
○ Outdoors

BEST FOR ADVENTURE:
SOUTH AMERICA

With mountains to climb, rivers to raft, ancient ruins to uncover and jungles to explore, South America is the ultimate adventure destination. Don't let its size daunt you – whether you're looking to do a big trip or a short haul, South America is more conducive to solo travel than you may think.

Logistically, it makes sense for longer-term travellers to follow the Gringo Trail, the classic route that encompasses the continent's most popular destinations from north to south (and vice versa). This lends to plenty of opportunities to buddy up with other travellers heading in the same direction. At the very least, you're bound to bump into the same people more than once along the way. South America has one of the world's best hostel networks, many of which can organise tours and transport for you, which makes it easy for solos

to ease into the destination when they first arrive. While Spanish is the national language in all but three countries (Guyana, French Guiana and Suriname), English is more widely spoken these days, and locals are overwhelmingly friendly.

Key considerations for solo travellers
Language: A basic understanding of Spanish will give solo travellers a lot more confidence. Consider signing up for a few weeks of Spanish tuition in your first destination, which is a great way to get acclimatised.

© JAROD RAWSTHORNE / GETTY IMAGES

LEFT Watch Gaucho horsemen herding cattle at Argentinian ranches.
ABOVE Get the perfect view of Machu Picchu in Peru.

© PHILIP LEE HARVEY / LONELY PLANET

© PHILIP LEE HARVEY / LONELY PLANET

Safety: Travel in South America involves a degree of risk taking. Clue yourself up on potentially dangerous regions and activities to help you make more informed travel decisions.

Budget: Travelling in Argentina, Brazil, Chile and Uruguay can be as expensive as travelling in Western Europe. Travel in Colombia and Peru is a little cheaper, while your savings will stretch further in Bolivia.

Health: A yellow fever vaccination is required for travel to South America. Be vigilant in protecting yourself against mosquito-borne diseases.

LEFT Spot sleepy Galápagos sea lions at Puerto Ayora and marine iguanas in groups relaxing on the islands' beaches.

Books for your Backpack

Lonely Planet's South America travel guides; *Latin American Spanish Phrasebook and Dictionary*, by Lonely Planet

≫→

The Motorcycle Diaries by Che Guevara

≫→

Inca-Kola by Matthew Parris

≫→

The House of the Spirits by Isabel Allende

GALAPAGOS ON A BUDGET

≫→ Thought cruising Ecuador's Galápagos Islands was out of reach for solo travellers? Think again. Many cruise companies offer the opportunity to share a berth with another solo traveller – and sometimes solos score the whole room to themselves if nobody else books the other bunk. If you have time to spare, head straight to the capital Quito to score a last-minute deal – travellers are rarely left waiting more than a few days to secure a berth for as much as 50% off (typically a saving of more than US$1000). Choose a standard boat that sleeps around 16 passengers, as they create an intimate environment perfect for getting to know your shipmates.

© JESS KRAFT / 500PX

ABOVE The tropical hues of Cartagena in Colombia are a photographer's dream.

Taking a 4WD tour from San Pedro de Atacama in Chile to Uyuni in Bolivia, traversing desert moonscapes and taking silly selfies at the salt flats. Tours rarely leave until vehicles are full so bank on doing this tour with others.

—

Watching the sunrise over Machu Picchu in Peru, whether you hiked or took the train from Cusco.

—

Mountain biking down Bolivia's infamous Death Road and debriefing with your fellow riders over a few beers afterwards.

—

Wandering the cobblestoned streets of Cartagena, Colombia, photographing the city's pastel-hued beauty.

SWEET STAYS

★ With five large hostels across three countries, **Loki** (named after the trickster Norse god) is a sure bet for solo travellers keen to meet new people (and party). Loki Cusco in Peru is housed in a beautiful 16th century building, while Loki La Paz in Bolivia boasts a glass-walled sky bar. (lokihostel.com)

★ If you're on a budget but prefer having your own room, try **El Viajero**, a 'poshtel' in the beautiful Colombian coastal city of Cartagena. This super-central, air-conditioned retreat is the only hostel in town with breakfast included, and offers a great roster of nightly activities. (elviajerohostels.com)

TOP TIP

Avoid rip-offs by asking your accommodation staff how much things should cost (such as taxi rides to tourist sights) before you head out for the day.

Practicalities

🧳 The Vietnamese tend to dress more modestly than locals in many other Southeast Asian countries. Take their lead and leave your mini-shorts and navel-baring tops at home.

✈ Ho Chi Minh City and Hanoi

LGBT-friendly ★★★☆☆

📅 Prices increase by up to 50% during the July to August high season, when the country is hot and humid. The December to March shoulder season brings clear skies to the south and cool conditions to the north, while the low season (April to June and September to November) is a great time to visit inland destinations as typhoons ravage the coast.

$ ▢▢▢▢

ABOVE Vietnam's floating markets proffer some of the country's best photo opportunities.

BEST FOR FOOD: VIETNAM

Don't tell Thailand, but if there is one Southeast Asian food nation to rule them all, it's Vietnam. Subtle in its flavours and outstanding in its diversity, Vietnamese cooking is a huge draw for travellers, the nation's myriad street-food tours and cooking schools making it ideal for solo travel.

- ◯ Culture
- ⬤ Food & Drink
- ◯ Adventure

© MATT MUNRO / LONELY PLANET

All over the country, you can mingle with villagers, sample local dishes and sip rice wine in Vietnam's many regional markets – head to major tourist centres including Hanoi, Ho Chi Minh City and Hoi An for the best range of foodie activities.

The long, skinny country makes a north-to-south (or vice versa) itinerary make sense – consider purchasing an 'open tour' bus ticket between Ho Chi Minh and Hanoi, and work your way up or down the country at your own pace. When you need some time out, head to one of the country's outstanding spas – from marble temples of treatments to simple family-run massage salons with backpacker-friendly rates.

Key considerations for solo travellers

Language: Many locals in tourist centres will speak some English, but a lot will speak none, so you may have to resort to hand gestures and picture pointing at times. Don't let this stress you out – almost every other traveller will be in the same boat.

Safety: Snatch-and-grab robberies are common in Vietnam; keep your daypack or handbag close to your body, and ensure your belongings are secured when riding a bicycle or motorbike. Do your research to help avoid scams.

Health: Serious health issues typically require evacuation to Thailand; ensure your travel insurance will cover you, and pay particular attention to your personal hygiene to help prevent contracting bugs.

Books for your Backpack

Lonely Planet's travel guides to Vietnam; *Vietnamese Phrasebook and Dictionary,* by Lonely Planet

≫→

The Quiet American by Graham Greene

Catfish and Mandala by Andrew Pham

≫→

When Heaven and Earth Changed Places by Le Ly Hayslip

© MATT MUNRO / LONELY PLANET

LEFT AND BELOW Vietnamese chefs make cooking complex local delicacies so easy...

SWEET STAYS

★ With an emphasis on good times and meeting other travellers, **The Hideout Hostel Saigon** is the place to stay in Ho Chi Minh City if you want to party. Dorms are spick and span, and you'll get a free beer each day at The Hideout Bar next door. The hostel also runs pub crawls six nights a week. There's a second branch (The Hangout Hostel Saigon) nearby, and another property, Phuong Le Villa, in Hoi An. (hideouthostels.asia)

★ For a posh pad near the action in Hanoi, it doesn't get better than **La Siesta Hotel & Spa**. On top of excellent service and quality, modern rooms, the hotel has a cracker location on Ma May St with scores of restaurants, bars and things to do on your very doorstep. After a big night out dodging motorbikes, you can chill out in the day spa or in the movie room. (hanoilasiestahotel.com)

HEAD FOR THE HiLLS

⟫⟶ Nervous solo female travellers interested in visiting the misty hill station of Sapa, Vietnam's ethnic minority tourism hub, would be wise to check out Sapa Sisters (sapasisters.com). Run by a group of savvy and knowledgeable Hmong women, the collective offers customised private day hikes and longer village homestay treks, staying and cooking with your guide – perfect for women travellers who feel more comfortable travelling with a female guide.

Epic Solo Travel Experiences

Learning how to cook a Vietnamese feast; highly recommended is Hoi An's Green Bamboo Cooking School (greenbamboo-hoian.com).

—

Taking moto-taxis everywhere, always with passenger helmets.

—

Learning about Vietnam's epoch-defining conflict at the Vietnam Military History Museum in Hanoi, the War Remnants Museum in Ho Chi Minh City, and at the Cu Chi tunnels north of Ho Chi Minh.

—

Taking an organised day trip or overnight tour from Hanoi to Halong Bay. The dramatic limestone pillars do draw in the crowds, but it's still spectacular.

TOP TIP

Eat, Pray, Love fans may be interested to know that healer Wayan Nuriasih, who starred in the hit film, still operates in Ubud.

Practicalities

✈ Denpasar, Bali

LGBT-friendly ★★★★☆

🧳 You'll be glad you left some room in your suitcase when you get to Ubud, which is packed with artisan boutiques. For textiles, don't miss Threads of Life Indonesian Textile Arts Center (threadsoflife.com).

📅 Ubud's dry season runs from May through September; although it can still rain, you'll have the best conditions for rural walks. While it is slightly wetter than the dry season, April and October sees vastly reduced crowds. Like much of the most popular parts of Bali, Ubud books up in August.

$ ▢ ▢ ▢ ▢

○ Culture

○ Relaxation

○ Food & Drink

BEST FOR SELF-REFLECTION:
UBUD, INDONESIA

Whether you loved or loathed Elizabeth Gilbert's famous solo travel memoir Eat, Pray, Love, *there's no denying it: Bali's artistic and spiritual centre – where the author found love – remains a wonderful place for solo travellers to relax, reflect and recharge.*

Nestled among emerald rice fields ringed by misty mountains, Ubud is a magical place. It is busier these days, yes, but the crowds can be easily avoided. Take a stroll to Ubud Palace, the home of Bali's royal family, that roughly marks its centre – and, to really harness the healing power of Ubud, check yourself into one of the many health retreats that dot the verdant hills surrounding the village. At the very least, indulge in an afternoon at one of the town's many day spas. Ubud's holistic vibe also spills over into its diverse and high-quality culinary offerings, with plenty of organic, vegetarian and vegan options among its juice bars, cafes and restaurants. Solo travel is so common in Ubud that the probing questions and curious glances that may be directed at lone travellers elsewhere in Bali are practically unheard of here – most visitors will find the local community is incredibly welcoming.

LEFT Soak up the serenity of Ubud's many moss-covered temples and shrines.

Key considerations for solo travellers

Language: English is

widely spoken in Ubud, but locals will appreciate your efforts to learn a few common Indonesian phrases. Start with *selamat pagi* (good morning) and *terimah kasih* (thank you).

Health: Due to years of being fed and provoked by humans, the band of 600-odd macaques that inhabit Ubud's Sacred Monkey Forest Sanctuary can be aggressive. While these monkeys are said to be free of rabies, the fatal disease is a risk across the island.

Local customs: You'll see plenty of travellers wearing short shorts and strappy tops in Ubud, but this is a holy place where more conservative dress should be observed, especially when visiting temples.

RIGHT Ubud's emerald rice paddies are full of walking tracks.
BELOW Keep your distance from Ubud's cute but unpredictable macaques.

© MATT MUNRO / LONELY PLANET

SCALING BALI'S HOLIEST PEAK

≫→ Towering over 3000m above sea level, Gunung Agung has enormous spiritual significance to the Balinese people, and climbing it is an important part of many visitors' spiritual journey to Ubud. Dawn hikes are easily organised in Ubud or online (try balisunrisetours.com); most ascents begin from either Pura Pasar Agung (1700m), from where it's a steep, three-to-four-hour climb through forest and volcanic scree to the summit for exquisite dawn views across to the neighbouring island of Lombok; or from Pura Besakih (Bali's holiest temple, which sits at an elevation of about 1000m), from where it's a less steep but longer six-hour haul.

Traipsing around Ubud's art museums and galleries; the Neka Art Museum, Museum Puri Lukisan and the Agung Rai Museum of Art.

—

Taking in a Balinese dance performance at a theatre after temple hopping around the city; visit the Ubud Tourist Information on Jl Raya Ubud.

—

Discovering why Ubud is one of Bali's hottest culinary capitals with a dinner at Locavore (locavore.co.id), a temple for local-sourced food.

—

Indulging in holistic offerings, from yoga to reiki at Taksu Healing Haven (taksuspa.com).

SWEET STAYS

★ One of the world's top health retreats, **Como Shambhala Estate** offers comprehensive wellness programs, perfect for serious inner searching in ultimate comfort. Set in gorgeous grounds outside the bustle of Ubud, the longstanding resort has a holy spring and two restaurants. (comoshambhala.com)

★ If you're thinking about taking some classes at Ubud's famed **The Yoga Barn**, why not stay there? The wellness centre has a lovely on-site guesthouse with private rooms and a four-bed dorm that tends to attract an international mix of solo travellers and small groups. (theyogabarn.com)

Practicalities

✈ Berlin (Tegel and Schönefeld Airports)

LGBT- friendly ★★★★★

💼 Berlin might be cheap, but make sure you always have enough cash to pay – cash is king in Germany and many establishments in Berlin do not accept cards.

📅 July and August are busiest, and warm but often rainy. May, June, September and October offer plenty of festivals, a more authentic experience and cooler, though often more stable, weather. Winters are cold and quiet.

$ $

○ Nightlife
○ Culture
○ Food & Drink

BEST FOR NIGHTLIFE:
BERLIN, GERMANY

Berlin is the ultimate place to party. It's also one of the friendliest, most inclusive cities in Europe, making it a fantastic place to hit the town as a solo traveller.

ABOVE The night comes alive in Berlin. RIGHT Dilapidated chic makes up the city's street scene.

Some say you are more likely to get into Berghain, the city's most famous nightclub, if you queue on your own, while Berlin's summer beer gardens offer great opportunities to make new friends over a few steins.

But there's more to this gritty-glam metropolis. Join a walking tour or set out on foot to visit key sights, from the Brandenburg Gate to the Holocaust Memorial, before losing yourself in Museumsinsel (Museum Island). The city is packed with alternative sights, from street art-emblazoned alleyways to abandoned buildings, quirky cafes, cool boutiques, weekend flea markets, and a growing food cart scene to explore.

Key considerations for solo travellers

Local customs: Berlin is a biker's city – pedestrians should avoid walking on biking pathways (usually coloured red) as cyclists usually travel at speed and have right of way. Injuries resulting from collisions between cyclists and pedestrians are common.

Safety: Berlin is one of Europe's safer cities, though foreign offices warn that the threat of terrorism remains high in Berlin following a December 2016 attack on a local Christmas market.

Language: Although English is widely understood in Berlin, English translations are not always available. Brushing up on a few common phrases will help to make your trip more seamless.

THE SOLO TRAVEL HANDBOOK

© LOOK DIE BILDAGENTUR DER FOTOGRAFEN GMBH / ALAMY STOCK PHOTO

RIGHT Night markets
are great places for solo
travellers to pick up a
quick dinner.

© MXRBERLIN / GETTY IMAGES

LEFT Berlin's riverside bars are the place to socialise during the summer months.

SWEET STAYS

★ It might not be Berlin's fanciest hostel, but **Jetpak Alternative** is arguably the best for solos. Aimed specifically at people travelling on their own or in small groups, the hostel in Kreuzberg (where many of the city's nightclubs are located) doesn't accept bookings for more than four people. The hostel attracts a friendly, alternative crowd, and its small common area has a great communal vibe. (jetpakberlin.com)

★ If you'd rather stay somewhere more central and comfortable, try **Casa Camper.** Right in the middle of downtown Mitte, this slick boutique hotel offers complimentary snacks and drinks around the clock at its top-floor common room Tentempié – the perfect environment to meet people. (casacamper.com). There's a 24-hour gym and sauna, too.

REVISITING BERLIN'S DARK PAST

≫⟶ It's not for everyone, but, for many, visiting a Nazi concentration camp provides an essential background to Germany's past and present. Sachsenhausen Concentration Camp, the first purpose-built camp established under SS Commander Heinrich Himmler, lies just outside Berlin, with many local tour companies offering day tours from the city. In 2012, the camp was opened as a museum and a memorial, its facilities renovated to provide an even more realistic idea of the brutal conditions of the camp, where more than 50,000 people lost their lives before it was liberated by the Soviets in 1945.

Epic Solo Travel Experiences

Heading out to a bar or nightclub and seeing where the night takes you.

—

Seeing the sights while mingling on a free walking tour of the city offered by Original Berlin Tours (originalberlintours.com).

—

Exploring the street art; head to Kreuzberg and Friedrichshain for the East Side Gallery, a section of the Berlin Wall.

—

Eating your way around Berlin's street food scene; visit timeout.com/berlin for the latest pop-ups.

—

Spending a weekend exploring flea markets, including Mauerpark and Boxhagener Platz.

THE SOLO TRAVEL HANDBOOK

TOP TIP

Snap like crazy: it's easy to get swept up in the magic of a safari and forget to take enough photos.

BEST FOR A GROUP TOUR:
EAST AFRICA

Have you always dreamed of viewing gorillas in the jungles of Rwanda, meeting a Maasai chief in Kenya, or spotting the 'big five' in Tanzania – but lack the confidence to travel to East Africa independently? A group tour is a great way to make your dream a reality.

While East Africa's tourism infrastructure is more developed than that in many other parts of the continent, it's not always easy – or safe – to navigate public transport or self-drive, especially on your own. By opting for an organised tour, you can bypass this stress and simply enjoy yourself. Budget adventure tour operators such as Intrepid (intrepidtravel.com) and G Adventures (gadventures.com) typically include overland vehicle transport and camping accommodation. Guests are usually split into groups to assist with camp duties such as food preparation and washing dishes, which helps to build community atmosphere. This bucket-list kind of trip attracts a wide demographic of travellers young and old, so you're not likely to be the only solo traveller stuck with a bunch of couples, whichever operator you choose.

Key considerations for solo travellers

Safety: Travelling on a tour bumps up your safety big time, but don't forget to stay alert when you are exploring on your own. Exercising a high degree of caution is recommended while travelling in most East Africa nations due to the

© PHILIP LEE HARVEY / LONELY PLANET

LEFT Let's face it: camping is more fun in a group.
ABOVE Enjoy fireside yarns with fellow travellers.

GOING LUXE

⟫⟶ If you can afford it, arranging a private guided East Africa travel itinerary is a fantastic way to get under the skin of this fascinating region, away from the busy standard group tour pit-stops. Organise your trip through an expert solo travel operator, such as Expert Africa (expertafrica.com), which can place you at safari camps where you aren't likely to get stuck with honeymooning couples. Many solo travellers report that Tanzania safari camps cater to them particularly well.

risk of serious crime and terrorism. *Health:* Viruses can spread quickly between travellers packed into overland vehicles for days at a time, so it's wise to bring plenty of cold and flu medication. Unwell travellers are advised not to undertake gorilla hikes, as human infections can be fatal for the endangered apes. *Budget:* Most costs are covered on organised tours to East Africa, but don't forget to budget for optional activities, alcohol and tipping your guide, driver and cook.

© ROBERT PETERNEL / 500PX

Books for your Backpack

Lonely Planet's travel guides to East Africa;
***Africa Phrasebook and Dictionary* by Lonely Planet**

⟫⟶

***Going Solo* by Roald Dahl**

⟫⟶

***Gorillas in the Mist* by Dian Fossey**

⟫⟶

***A Grain of Wheat* by Ngugi wa Thiong'o**

RIGHT Pack a pair of binoculars to help you spot game that isn't as bold as this fella.

© MICHAEL HEFFERNAN / LONELY PLANET

© RENATO GRANIERI / ALAMY STOCK PHOTO

SWEET STAYS

★ Starting your tour in Nairobi, Kenya? Consider acclimatising for a few nights at **Wildebeest Eco Camp**, which offers deluxe, tented accommodation at a fraction of the price of typical safari camps. The property is set in a lush garden, with a year-round swimming pool and a fantastic communal fireplace. You can take all your meals here, too. (wildebeestecocamp.com)

★ If you're looking to build in some beach days at the end of your trip, check out **Drifters Backpackers** in Paje, one of Zanzibar's most popular beach towns. The hostel is run by travellers, for travellers, and offers a clean, secure and friendly place to bed down just steps from beautiful Paje Beach. Its barbecue nights are legendary. (facebook.com/driftersbackpackers)

Epic Solo Travel Experiences

Viewing gorillas in Rwanda. Permits are pre-arranged for most groups; solo travellers should contact the Rwanda Development Board in advance. Stop by the Kigali Genocide Memorial en route.

—

Cruising past hippos, elephants and crocs along the Kazinga Channel in Uganda's Queen Elizabeth National Park.

—

Spotting big cats on a game drive through one of the many safari parks.

—

Visiting a Maasai tribe in Kenya with your tour group.

—

Chilling out on the white sand beaches of Zanzibar, Tanzania.

THE SOLO TRAVEL HANDBOOK

Singapore is one of the world's greenest cities

Practicalities

✈ Singapore

LGBT-friendly ★★✩✩✩

💼 A hat, sunscreen, a bottle of water and an umbrella are daypack essentials for pounding the steamy pavements of Singapore. Leave your chewing gum at home, which is illegal in the city-state.

📅 Singapore is tropical and humid year-round. School holidays fall in June, the hottest (and haziest) time, so try to avoid travelling then if possible.

$ $ $

BEST FOR A SOLO STOPOVER:
SINGAPORE

○ Food & Drink
○ Culture
○ Adventure

With one of the world's best public transport systems (including excellent airport links), a plethora of cultural attractions to explore, and mouth-wateringly delicious hawker food at every turn, it's difficult to pick an easier city for solo travel than Singapore.

It might be one of the world's most expensive cities, but there are plenty of ways to visit this vibrant Southeast Asian capital on the cheap.

A good handful of museums and galleries, including Baba House and Gillman Barracks, are free, while many others, including the Chinatown Heritage Centre and the Indian Heritage Centre, have excellent audio guides perfectly suited for solo travel. It also won't cost you a cent to wander around Singapore's fantastic green spaces, including Singapore Botanic Gardens and the outdoor gardens at the futuristic botanic fantasyland known as Gardens by the Bay.

Singapore's hostel offerings have improved over recent years, offering solo travellers more options to bed down in a social environment for a fraction of the price of a hotel, while the city's obsession with hawker food makes mealtimes a breeze. While the city-state has four official languages, you're unlikely to meet many locals who don't speak English.

Key considerations for solo travellers

Budget: Start saving! US$100/day will be lucky to get you a decent hostel bed, hawker centre meals, entry to at least one major museum and a couple of local beers.

Health: Singapore may be one of the world's cleanest countries, but dengue fever remains a risk (even in urban areas), so don't forget to pack insect repellent.

Local customs: While Singapore has a thriving gay scene, travellers should be mindful that sex between men is illegal.

THE SOLO TRAVEL HANDBOOK

TOP TIP

To reserve a table in a busy
hawker centre, simply leave
a packet of tissues on the
seat, which is Singapore
food-speak for "this
spot is mine."

© NEIL SETCHFIELD / ALAMY STOCK PHOTO

© IVAN TYKHYI / 500PX

ABOVE Singapore's architecture
spans modern malls to colourful
heritage buildings.

SWEET STAYS

★ **Adler Hostel** is a self-proclaimed 'poshtel' that boasts feather-down duvets and complimentary Malin+Goetz toiletries, perfect for solo travellers looking for a little more luxury than a standard hostel. Located in the centre of Chinatown, it's in easy reach of excellent hawker centres including the Chinatown Complex, where you can enjoy a Michelin-starred meal for as little as S$1.50 at the Hong Kong Soya Sauce Chicken Rice and Noodle stall. (adlerhostel.com)

★ For imaginative Singapore accommodation at its best, book a room at **Wanderlust Hotel**, where your abode could resemble anything from a tree house to a spaceship. This quirky boutique hotel in the colourful district of Little India has a ground-floor bar (and restaurant), perfect for socialising. (wanderlusthotel. com) and a good selection of digital magazines available to guests who connect to the in-house wi-fi network.

CYCLING PULAU UBIN

⫸→ If you need a break from the city bustle, take a step back into old-world Singapore on a self-guided day trip to Pulau Ubin. Located off Singapore's north coast (easily accessed by a bus and bumboat combination from the city), this sleepy, jungly isle is best explored by bicycle. Bikes are easily rented from several operators near the jetty. Make for Chek Jawa Wetlands at the island's eastern tip, which features a 1km coastal boardwalk, and the 20m-high Jejawi Tower – climb it for sweeping coastal views and a good chance of seeing monkeys swinging through the jungle canopy.

Epic Solo Travel Experiences

Discovering new haunts on a food tour offered by Betel Box (betelbox.com).

—

Wandering between museums and galleries, such as the new National Gallery Singapore.

—

Checking out the cafes and boutiques in the gentrified 1930s housing estate of Tiong Bahru.

—

Taking a stroll around the Marina Bay lit up at night.

—

Exploring Singapore's fascinating places of worship, from mosques and Chinese temples, to Anglican churches and Hindu shrines. Be sure to cover your shoulders and knees before you enter.

TOP TIP

Seek out Rome's aperitivo (happy hour) bars where buffet food is included in the price of a drink. Freni e Frizioni (freniefrizioni.com) in Trastevere is one of the best.

Practicalities

✈ Rome (Leonardo da Vinci-Fiumicino and Ciampino Airports)

LGBT-friendly ★★★★☆

🧳 Your feet will thank you for packing comfortable sandals or sneakers. Shoulder- and knee-covering clothes are required for visits to Vatican City, including St Peter's Basilica.

📅 June through August sees the heaviest tourist traffic in Rome. Aim for the shoulder seasons (April to June and September to October), which offer good weather but fewer crowds.

$ ▢ ▢ ▢ ▢

○ Culture
◐ Food & Drink
◉ Outdoors

BEST FOR CULTURE:
ROME

If you've always dreamed of travelling to Italy and can't wait any longer for a travel buddy to join you, Rome is the perfect place to start your solo travel adventure. It might be a big, busy city, but you'll never feel like a fish out of water among the 14 million-odd other tourists that visit this cultural hub each year.

From ancient icons like the Colosseum and the Roman Forum to the towering masterpiece of Renaissance architecture that is St Peter's Basilica, Rome's cityscape is an exhilarating spectacle. Whether you're visiting for two days or two weeks, there is so much to see that there is little risk of ever becoming bored.

Rome has decent public transport, but this is a walker's city – if you've got the stamina, almost all essential sights can be explored on foot. Arm yourself with a good map, but don't tune your itinerary too finely, allowing yourself the flexibility to take time out for espresso, gelato, *vino* and pizza *al taglio* (by the slice) between exploring ornate piazzas and elaborate churches. Getting lost is half the fun of exploring Rome. Don't be embarrassed to ask for directions – you won't be the first solo traveller to be swept up in the magic of The Eternal City.

Key considerations for solo travellers

Language: It may surprise some travellers to learn that English is not as widely spoken in Rome as you may think.

© NICO DE PASQUALE PHOTOGRAPHY / GETTY IMAGES

LEFT Take your sweet time to explore the majestic Roman Forum.
RIGHT Avoid the crowds by visiting the Trevi Fountain in the evening.

© ANDREA CALANDRA / 500PX

Books for your Backpack

Lonely Planet's travel guides to Rome; *Italian Phrasebook and Dictionary* by Lonely Planet

≫⟶

A Day in the Life of Ancient Rome by Alberto Angela

≫⟶

Rome Tales edited by Helen Constantine

≫⟶

The Roman Spring of Mrs. Stone by Tennessee Williams

Brushing up on common phrases (as well as hand gestures – Italians are thought to use around 250 each day) will come in handy. *Safety:* Rome is a safe city but petty theft can be a problem, and pickpockets are active in touristy areas and on crowded public transport. Use common sense and watch your valuables. *Overcoming loneliness:* Set yourself up for a great opportunity to meet people while discovering the hidden corners of Rome (such as the city's crypts and catacombs) on a walking tour with the likes of Walks of Italy (walksofitaly.com).

COOKING UP A STORM

≫⟶ If there's one activity every trip to Italy should include, it's a cooking class. The options are plentiful in Rome; for a more personal experience, opt for a class with local cook David Sgueglia della Marra, who takes students shopping at Rome's Campo de' Fiori market in the morning for ingredients which they will learn how to whip into a four-course lunch at his Piazza Argentina loft. If you'd rather explore the city by day, Sgueglia della Marra also offers an evening class which begins with a cocktail hour before the group learns how to make fresh pasta (acookingdayinrome.com).

Visiting St Peter's Basilica and walking the 7km of halls that comprise the Vatican Museums.

—

Exploring the Roman Forum; skip the queues and purchase entry tickets in advance at coopculture.it.

—

Enjoying an evening out in the buzzing Trastevere district.

—

Savouring *la dolce vita* over a perfect espresso – Sant'Eustachio il Caffè is said to serve the best coffee in town.

—

Tossing a coin into the famous Trevi Fountain, thus ensuring – according to tradition – that you will return to Rome.

SWEET STAYS

★ When it comes to hostels in Rome, it doesn't get much better than **Generator Rome**. Spread across seven floors, this design-savvy 'poshtel' in the lively Monti neighbourhood has 12 four-bed dorms and 53 private rooms, anchored by a beautiful old Havana-themed bar and chill-out lounge, perfect for mingling. (generatorhostels.com)

★ Just two blocks from Roma Termini Station, **The Beehive** also has dorms and private rooms, yet this cosy eco-conscious hostel feels more like a guesthouse. After a long day pounding the cobblestoned streets of Rome, relax in one of three charming 'comfort zones' (including an on-site cafe) with fellow guests. (the-beehive.com)

TOP TIP

Portland is one of America's rainier cities, but there are plenty of interesting places to escape the drizzle. Check out the Shanghai Tunnels (shanghaitunnels.info), where in the late 19th and early 20th centuries, local men were kidnapped and sold to passing ships as slaves.

Practicalities

✈ Portland

LGBT-friendly ★★★★☆

💼 Portland's dress code is very relaxed; relish the opportunity to adopt adventurewear as your uniform.

📅 Portland really comes alive during the summer months (June to September), with festivals galore. But the city is a year-round travel destination, with plenty of museums, coffee shops and brewpubs to keep you busy during the cooler months.

$ $ ☐ ☐ ☐

○ Food & Drink
○ Outdoors
○ Culture

BEST FOR A CITY BREAK:
PORTLAND, OREGON, USA

One of America's coolest cities, Portland has all the cultural advantages of a major city, but the feel of a small town. Also one of America's greenest cities – literally and figuratively – it's a top spot for conscientious solo travellers looking to take a more sustainable city break.

With more than a dozen urban wineries, not to mention a microbrewery and coffee roaster at every turn, Portland is a drinkers' paradise. But there's plenty more to this bastion of counterculture, from a museum dedicated to vacuum cleaners to an urban herd of goats you can visit in the Lents District. Hugging the Willamette River, Portland might be Oregon's largest city, but this compact metropolis is easy to get around on foot, via the city's excellent public transport network, or by utilising Biketown, Portland's bike-share system. And while the city is famous for its artisan restaurants, it has more than 500 food carts available at any given time, which makes mealtimes so much fun for solos. Most carts stay put in groups dubbed 'pods,' making it a snap to sample several at a time. And did we mention Portland's tax-free shopping?

Key considerations for solo travellers

Safety: Portland is one of America's safer cities, but it is not advised to walk around alone at night downtown or in the industrial southeast; save the number of a local taxi company into your phone as cabs can't usually be flagged down in the street.

© JOSHUA RAINEY PHOTOGRAPHY / SHUTTERSTOCK

LEFT Mt Hood crowns Portland's dazzling skyline.
ABOVE You're spoiled for choice when it comes to food trucks in Portland.

BELOW The great outdoors reigns supreme in Portland.

OUTDOOR ADVENTURES GALORE

≫⟶ Portland is the perfect launchpad for outdoor activities and adventure. Northwest of the city centre, Forest Park boasts more than 129km (80 miles) of trails including the Wildwood Trail, a National Recreation Trail which connects historic Pittock Mansion, Hoyt Arboretum and the Audubon Wildlife Sanctuary. Fans of falling water should not miss the breathtaking Columbia River Gorge waterfalls east of the city; it's easy to self-drive, or you can sign up for a day trip with a local operator like Evergreen Escapes (evergreenescapes.com).

Overcoming loneliness: Weary of dining alone? For a non-intimidating night out, head to one of Portland's famed brew 'n' view theatres, where you can enjoy a proper dinner (think: artisan pizza and a microbrew) and a flick.

Local customs: Portland was among the first US cities to ban plastic bags. Come prepared by bringing your own reusable carry bag – bonus points if you bring your reusable coffee cup, too.

© ERIK ISAKSON / GETTYIMAGES

Books for your Backpack

Lonely Planet's travel guides to Washington, Oregon and the Pacific Northwest

≫⟶

Fugitives and Refugees: A Walk in Portland, Oregon by Chuck Palahniuk

≫⟶

Geek Love by Katherine Dunn

≫⟶

Lean on Pete by Willy Vlautin

© JAMIE FRANCIS / TRAVEL PORTLAND

ABOVE If you love
a brewery tour (or
two), Portland has
you sorted.

© TRAVEL PORTLAND

Working your way around
the city's food carts.
Sign up for a tour with
Food Carts Portland
(foodcartsportland.com).

—

Browsing Powell's City
of Books. Occupying
almost an entire city block,
it's the world's largest
independent bookstore.

—

Wandering Portland's
gardens; don't miss the
century-old International
Rose Test Garden.

—

Exploring the Alberta Arts
District; time your visit
to coincide with the Last
Thursday art walk.

—

Visiting brewery spots
on a tour with Brewvana
(brewvana.com).

SWEET STAYS

★ Stay in one of six
adorable custom-
built tiny houses at **Caravan**,
located in Portland's Alberta
Arts District. The caravans are
positioned around a central
gathering space, with free
s'mores nightly around the fire
pit. There are plenty of excellent
dining options within walking
distance, but each tiny house is
equipped with cooking facilities
should you prefer to eat in.
(tinyhousehotel.com)

★ Literally a home
away from home,
Travelers' House is an
independent hostel set in a
thoughtfully renovated house,
1500m west of Caravan. A
community vibe reigns at this
incredibly welcoming place,
which actively encourages
guests to engage with each
other – off the premises
after 10pm, so other guests
can get a good night's sleep.
(travelershouse.org)

Practicalities

✈ Ladyville, Belize; Chetumal and Cancún, Mexico.

LGBT-friendly ★★★☆☆

💼 If you love lobster, time your trip to coincide with July's Lobsterfest, which offers visitors the chance to taste every lobster dish imaginable (yes, even lobster ice cream).

📅 December to April for clear skies but peak crowds; November and May for mostly dry but humid weather and fewer tourists. Hurricanes are a risk between June and November, which also sees heavy rainfall.

$ ▢▢▢▢

BEST FOR A TROPICAL ISLAND ESCAPE:
CAYE CAULKER, BELIZE

◯ Beach
◉ Relaxation
◉ Food & Drink

You don't have to be on honeymoon to holiday on a tropical island. Especially when that island is Caye Caulker – one of the prettiest, most friendly isles in Central America (if not the entire Caribbean), with world-class diving and snorkelling on its sandy doorstep.

LEFT Which brightly coloured beach bungalow has your name on it?

© MATTEO COLOMBO / GETTY IMAGES

© SIMON VELAZQUEZ / 500PX

© LEANNE WALKER / GETTY IMAGES

ABOVE Swing in a hammock or grab your snorkel: it's your choice.

Just a short ferry ride from Belize City or the Mexican state of Quintana Roo, this pastel-hued, car-free isle has always been a great place for solo travellers thanks to its compact size and easy-going, backpacker-friendly vibe, which tends to attract a relaxed, international crowd. It's easy to lose days hanging out at The Split, the island's main beach, but there are plenty of other activities on offer, from snorkelling and diving over Technicoloured reefs, to kayaking around the lesser-visited parts of the island, keeping a beady eye out for crocs! Join other travellers at local reggae bars during the afternoon happy hour before moving on to local restaurants or street food stands to fill your belly with lip-smacking Creole cuisine.

Key considerations for solo travellers

Safety: While most solo travellers report feeling safe on Caye Caulker, getting there may require transiting through Belize City, which has a bad reputation for violent crime. Avoid walking around alone at night in the capital, and on quiet streets at night on Caye Caulker.

Health: When this book went to press, the Zika virus was present in Belize – don't forget to lather up with insect repellent. This will also protect you from sand flies that are present on some beaches.

Budget: Belize tends to be a little pricier than other countries in Central America. If you dream of diving Belize's Great Blue Hole, which is possible from Caye Caulker, expect to pay around US$260.

133

THE SOLO TRAVEL HANDBOOK

Lonely Planet's travel
guides to Belize

➤➤➤

Beka Lamb by Zee Edgell

➤➤➤

*The Last Flight of the
Scarlet Macaw*
by Bruce Barcott

➤➤➤

How to Cook a Tapir
by Joan Fry

TOP TIP

Bring your own
snorkel and fins to
save money on
rental fees.

© PNIESSEN / GETTY IMAGES

© SARAH REID

Budget Man
Special
Stew Conch
Jerk Lobster
Curry Pork
Coconut white rice
Stewed Veggies
Fried Plantains

LEFT A loggerhead sea turtle glides through turquoise waters near Caye Caulker.
LEFT Feast on local street food delights along the shore.

SWEET STAYS

★ Easily the nicest (and quietest) hostel on the island, brightly painted **Yuma's House Belize** is just a few steps from the taxi dock. It has a guest kitchen, a private dock and a lovely palm-shaded, hammock-strewn garden perfect for socialising over a few local Belikin beers. Guests wanting to party would be wise to head to Dirty McNasty's Hostel nearby. (yumashousebelize.com)

★ For a little more luxury, try **Seaside Cabanas Hotel.** Guestrooms in the sun-yellow main building are set around a lovely pool with plenty of sun loungers, making it a great spot to meet people. If you prefer your privacy, opt for a beachfront cabana; each has a personal rooftop hot tub. (seasidecabanas.com)

JOURNEY TO THE MAINLAND

⟫→ If you fancy a diversion from island life, consider a day trip to the mainland to find out what Belize has to offer beyond its idyllic islands. A good handful of options are available from Caye Caulker (check out tsunamiadventures.com), from trips to the ancient Mayan ruins of Lamanai, which was hidden in the jungle until excavation works began in the 1970s, to tubing tours down the Sibun River, known as Belize's 'river of caves'. You may have to wait for at least one other person to book for a tour to go ahead, so put your name down on the first day you arrive for the best chance of getting on a confirmed departure.

Epic Solo Travel Experiences

Lazing on the sand at The Split, a beach formed by a hurricane that split Caye Caulker in two. The adjacent Lazy Lizard Bar provides the beats and the beers.

—

Snorkelling or diving in the Caye Caulker Marine Reserve, which teems with turtles and sharks.

—

Sipping rum on a sunset cruise around the island with Raggamuffin Tours (raggamuffintours.com).

—

Spotting manatees in Swallow Caye Wildlife Sanctuary on a day trip.

—

Sampling delicious Creole street food; fish, chicken and lobster all grilled by friendly locals.

TOP TIP

Dining on a budget? Make sure to look for Thai restaurants, Australia's answer to UK Indian curry houses and US Chinese takeaway joints.

✈ Sydney, New South Wales; Brisbane, Cairns and the Gold Coast, Queensland.

LGBT-friendly ★★★★☆

💼 Australia experiences some of the highest levels of UV radiation in the world; Cancer Council Australia recommends using a sunscreen that is labelled SPF30 or above.

📅 For summer accommodation (December to February) book ahead. Temperatures can drop to single digits in Sydney during June, July and August, the most pleasant time to visit Far North Queensland.

$ $ $

○ Adventure
○ Outdoors
○ Beach

BEST FOR ROAD-TRIPPING:
EAST COAST AUSTRALIA

From dazzling coastal capitals and sleepy fishing towns, to spectacular national parks and seemingly endless deserted beaches, East Coast Australia is a stunner. The classic road trip from Sydney to Cairns is also one of the world's easiest to pull off as a solo traveller.

Driving along Australia's stunning east coast is a cinch. Simply follow the highway that snakes its way along the nation's eastern perimeter, just inland from the coast, making detours through coastal towns and inland villages along the way as you please. Rarely will you need to drive for more than half an hour to reach a fuel station or a supermarket, and there are dozens of fantastic camping grounds to overnight at along the way, where you are bound to meet other travellers.

If you don't fancy driving at all, there are solid bus connections between key tourism hubs including Sydney, Byron Bay, Gold Coast, Brisbane, Noosa, Airlie Beach and Cairns. As dusk falls, look out for wallabies and kangaroos grazing by the roadside. Travel between May and November for the best chances of travelling up or down the coast alongside migrating whales.

Key considerations for solo travellers

Budget: Australia is expensive. Expect to pay around AU$35 for a bed in a shared dorm on the East Coast. It's roughly

LEFT Watch the sun rise from the Cape Byron Lighthouse.
RIGHT Zoom along Fraser Island's beaches on a 4WD tour.

Lonely Planet's travel guides
to East Coast Australia

≫⟶

Australia's Best Trips
by Lonely Planet

≫⟶

Puberty Blues by Gabrielle
Carey and Kathy Lette

≫⟶

The Harp in the South
by Ruth Park

≫⟶

*Down Under/In a Sunburned
Country* by Bill Bryson

the same price per day to hire a camper (try hippiecamper.com). Self-catering can help to keep costs down, while Australia's small-town bakeries are legendary for their freshly baked cheap treats. *Overcoming loneliness:* If you're self-driving and camping, social interaction can be limited. If you fancy some company, research hostels in each destination that run activities for non-guests, and keep an eye on gig guides for local pubs. *Safety:* Australian beaches are among the world's most dangerous; always swim between the red-and-yellow flags, and never swim alone if you're a weak swimmer, or unable to identify hazardous surf conditions such as rips.

© KYLE TAYLOR / 500PX

© SUZANNE MARSHALL / GETTY IMAGES

iSLAND ADVENTURE

≫⟶ It wouldn't be a trip to East Coast Australia without a detour to Fraser Island. This UNESCO-listed sand island – the world's largest – is the ultimate Australian wilderness destination. Avoid the risk of damaging a rental car on Fraser's wild sandy roads by joining a multi-day camping safari tour (try dropbearadventures.com.au) on which you can enjoy island highlights such as swimming in the crystal-clear waters of Lake McKenzie, visiting the crumbling Maheno shipwreck, driving through towering Aussie bush, and spotting the island's most famous species: the dingo.

© FRANCESCO RICCARDO IACOMINO / GETTY IMAGES

ABOVE East Coast Australia's deserted beaches and idyllic islands beg you to dive in.

RIGHT See Sydney from a different angle on the Sydney Harbour Bridge Climb.

Epic Solo Travel Experiences

Rolling out your beach towel on Sydney's iconic Bondi Beach and strolling along to Bronte Beach.

—

Learning to surf in Byron Bay; there are plenty of surf schools to choose from.

—

Exploring the quaint villages and stunning waterfalls that dot the far NSW north coast hinterland by car.

—

Day-tripping to the Great Barrier Reef; book through a hostel in Cairns or Airlie Beach for a good chance to meet other travellers.

—

Hiking through the ancient emerald abyss of the Daintree Rainforest, north of Cairns.

SWEET STAYS

★ Could there be any other hostel with a better view than **Sydney Harbour YHA**? With a great communal rooftop terrace boasting views across Sydney Harbour towards the Harbour Bridge, this slick hostel nestled in The Rocks, Sydney's most historic neighbourhood, is perfectly located for exploring top city sights on foot. (yha.com.au)

★ There are more than a thousand hostel beds in the iconic NSW surf town of Byron Bay, but if you prefer to avoid the party crowds in comfort, try **The Atlantic**. The communal spaces at this stylish, central B&B – including a pool area, fire pit, guest kitchen and shaded deck areas – lend to a delightfully sociable atmosphere. (atlanticbyronbay.com.au)

THE SOLO TRAVEL HANDBOOK

INSPIRATION:
SOLO TRAVEL TALES

'WHAT A SNOWSHOEING TRIP

'A Christmastime trip to the Alps was one of many firsts for me: my first solo journey to Europe, my first time snowshoeing, and the first time I realised how being hooked to my smartphone could've landed me in a scary situation.

Having dwelled in hot and humid climes for most of my life, finding myself in a powdery winter wonderland during the holidays was a delight. Mountaineering of any sort was outside my wheelhouse; my experience with snow sports started (and ended) with skiing on the bunny slopes during a family vacation to Colorado when I was a teenager – it was an embarrassing, bruise-inducing conquest that was never attempted again.

But travelling all that way just to enjoy the snow from indoors wasn't going to suffice.

I had to get out into the wilderness and soak up the Alpine scenery... and snap some good pictures to post on Instagram. I couldn't be bothered to give skiing another go – and snowboarding was out of the question – so the owner of my hostel, Doug, encouraged me to give snowshoeing a shot.

There was a nearby trail that terminated at a slope-side lodge where I could pick up a solo sledge to get myself back down the mountain once I completed the route. Doug convinced me it'd all be a breeze and mentioned that a couple of other guests had just set off on the same trail about 15 minutes prior, and I was sure to catch up to them. Then he strapped what resembled compact skis to my feet; admittedly, when he presented the snowshoeing idea, I imagined I'd be sporting a more traditional, tennis racket-like pair constructed

TAUGHT ME ABOUT SOLO TRAVEL'

from wood. Doug snapped a quick photo of me in my gear at the trailhead and then sent me on my way to catch up with the others.

After 20 minutes of ambling along the trail, I realised that there wasn't another soul anywhere close by – the snow was so dense and still that it rendered the mountain silent, and it hadn't occurred to me before that moment to look on the ground for any tracks on the trail to confirm I wasn't completely alone in this wilderness. There were just enough signs posted to keep me moving in the right direction, so I embraced the solitude and feeling of smallness in the shadows of the peaks. I revelled inside my own private snow globe, growing ever gleeful as I snapped photo after photo on my iPhone. There was zero shame in my selfie game – the only other living creatures I spotted were a doe and her fawn, both of which were unfazed by my narcissism and naivety.

To say I was ill prepared is a mortifying understatement. I didn't think to bring along a single necessity – no water, compass or map – besides the clothes on my back and mini skis on my feet, the only objects in my possession were my phone, a plastic toy camera and an extra roll of 35mm film that remained un-shot.

A route that was supposed to take about an hour had turned into a few hours. I found myself with a waning phone battery and no reception under a fast-setting afternoon sun.

Being completely entranced by the vastness and beauty around me, I knew as I trudged and tripped up those hills in a fury that I let the whims of technology undermine my common sense. I was a novice in so many ways, but most gravely of all, giving in to the impulse to document every scene at every turn cost me a lot of time. I chastised myself for failing to burn more of those astounding images into my memory, rather than my phone's camera roll, in order to make good time, and ultimately ensure my safe passage off this mountain.

My unsteady and stilted gait, fuelled by chanting words of self-encouragement, finally landed me at that mountainside lodge as the sun sank over the horizon. After an exchange of confused looks and a few indecipherable German phrases with a lodge attendant, I loaded my snowshoes onto the metal sledge built for one and shot downslope with a sigh of relief into the Bavarian dusk, vowing never to make such a silly mistake again.'

MASOVAIDA MORGAN,
LONELY PLANET DESTINATION EDITOR

'HOW MY FIRST SOLO TRIP

I was 21 when I took the trip that would change my life: a six-week solo adventure through Europe. I was going through a rough patch before I booked it; I was unhappy with my life and my relationship. A close family member had just passed away and I was devastated. I remember very clearly, sitting at my desk at work, trying to fight back tears. I was incredibly angry, frustrated, and overwhelmed by how unhappy I felt in my life. All I could think was, "I need something to happen in my life. I need something BIG." Without really thinking, I jumped on a flight booking website and found a sale on one-way airfares to Paris. I grabbed my credit card, hands shaking, and booked it.

Booking that flight was an incredibly exhilarating moment. It was the first time I'd really stood up and done something big for myself. I figured I'd just sort out the rest of my trip later and, when it came time, I booked myself on the longest group tour I could find, extending my stay with time in Paris and London. I didn't know it at the time, but I would end up meeting one of my best friends to this day, and have an adventure that would change my life forever.

Before I made a spur-of-the-moment decision to travel solo, I had a good crack at trying to convince friends to travel with me, but all I received was empty promises and false hopes. I realised I couldn't keep putting my life – and desire to travel – on hold, waiting for others to help me live the life I wanted. I had to take charge of my own destiny and be brave enough to go by myself.

I remember how I felt sitting in the airport alone, waiting for my

CHANGED EVERYTHING'

flight to leave for Paris, having just kissed my boyfriend (who wasn't able to travel with me at the time) goodbye, knowing I wouldn't see him for six weeks. I was overwhelmed with a mix of fear, anxiety and excitement about the adventure ahead of me. Twenty-four hours later, when I finally began to spot the tops of Parisian buildings come into view through the plane window, I (somewhat embarrassingly) started to cry. Thinking about it now, it must have been the stress leading up to that moment finally being released. I was just so happy to be there.

My trip took me to incredible places like London, Paris, Rome, Santorini and Dubrovnik, and it taught me so many things about myself, and about the world. It also gave me a huge amount of

clarity. I remember sitting on a rock in Meteora, Greece, having this strange sense of calm ripple through my body. Out of nowhere I realised, innately, that this is what I wanted in my life – to travel and find myself in moments like this one, tangled up in crazy, wild, fabulous adventures.

That moment propelled me to the place I am now, where my travel blog is my full-time job. It was my dream to be a travel writer but I didn't have the self-confidence or self-belief to go after it. My solo trip lit the fuse and helped me start to build the confidence I needed to go after my dreams. It also made my boyfriend and I realise we wanted to travel together, and now we're married and get to travel the world together capturing videos, photos and written content for the blog.

My first solo trip was inspired by fear, frustration and desperation. Now my travels are inspired by a love of adventure, an innate self-trust, and the value I put on my own happiness. It took nine years and a lot of hard work to get to this point, but I'm grateful I went through it all and learned everything I did. Most of all I'm glad I stopped waiting around for other people and decided to start relying on myself to be happy, because the moment I did, my whole life changed.'

PHOEBE LEE,
TRAVEL BLOGGER, LITTLEGREYBOX.COM

'THE UNINTENTIONAL SOLO TRIP

'As a chairlift operator unceremoniously hoisted me back to my feet and I clumsily jabbed at the snow with my ski poles, the only thing clearer than the bright spring sunshine glistening over Mayrhofen's magnificent whipped peaks was the white hot realisation that my mate Jon was an idiot.

I had first thought it back at Heathrow Airport when the airhostess had politely turned him away at the departure gate. We'd breezed through check-in, passed security and washed down a fry-up with a pint of beer before anyone had noticed that his passport was out of date. Now we stood just metres from the plane and Jon was being told that his bag would be taken out of the hold and he'd be escorted back through security.

We had planned to learn to ski at the Snowbombing music festival in the Alps. How hard could it be? We'd spur one another on and pick each other up when we fell. By the end of the week we'd be carving up red runs. Maybe even black! But ever since he sloped back to South London, I had become increasingly worried that I might only be spending time with my shadow. Who would I ski with? How would I make friends? Could I slug schnapps on my own?

So that's how I found myself alone at the top of an Austrian mountain, a crumpled blaze of second-hand neon. Falling chin-first from the chairlift as the safety bar lifted was merely a plump red cherry atop a three-tiered turd-cake of a day.

This wasn't a solo expedition of a great adventurer – I wasn't going to fearlessly hack at overgrown vines or drink my own urine to survive – but the prospect of being

THAT WAS A BLESSING IN DISGUISE'

alone was daunting. Just emerging from the jungle of the ski rental shop with armfuls of boots, poles, skis and a helmet felt like a victory.

But no good stories ever came from eating paprika crisps and channel-hopping in a cut-price hotel room, so I kitted up in enough thermal underwear to survive an Arctic apocalypse and wrangled an hour-long ski lesson on a nursery slope. Adventures begin when you bite the bullet and grinding my knee cartilage into soft spaghetti whilst learning to snow plough felt like chewing down on a cannonball.

An hour later I was rocking over the lip of a preposterously steep piste that led right off the edge of the mountain. Other skiers would saddle up next to me, loop the ski pole straps over their gloves, and schuss off into the abyss. I never imagined my last moments

on Earth would involve steamed-up ski goggles and Daft Punk's *One More Time* belting out from a nearby bar, but when poetry writes itself the inevitable tends to happen, so I darted downhill.

It turned out that red runs were pretty simple: once I'd mastered the sideways slump, things quickly progressed. Soon I could pull myself up using my poles; my skis would then sail downhill with my legs attached and I'd stop by falling over with a slow, dignified flump.

I was toasting my survival in the wood-panelled bar of my hotel when a woman in large, clear-framed glasses bundled in. Kara had a grin the size of Greenland and a similar story to mine. She was on her own for a couple of days too, so as you do in this part of the world, we ordered Jägerbombs to toast our new friendship.

In a matter of hours, we had amassed a legion of new pals including Northern Nick who had pulled off his t-shirt and whirled it over his head to a drum 'n' bass track in the sweaty pub. For the rest of the week we raved in sticky-floored clubs where the speakers would blow our eardrums and partied in an igloo where the bartender free-poured vodka down our throats.

Nick even taught me to ski – or as near as, damn it. That's the thing about solo travel: you're never actually on your own, you just don't know the names of your new mates yet. I had such a good time that I went off to Snowbombing by myself the following year and had just as much fun. Jon, meanwhile, still hasn't renewed his passport.'

DANIEL FAHEY,
LONELY PLANET DESTINATION EDITOR

THE SOLO TRAVEL HANDBOOK

'SOLO TRAVEL ISN'T ALWAYS MY

'I'll be the first to admit that travelling solo isn't always my first choice. I love travelling with my husband; in fact we've been to more than 60 countries together, and he is the best travel partner I've ever had. I love travelling with my two-year-old daughter even more – she shows me the world through new perspectives and adds new meaning to travel for me. But as a professional travel blogger and serial travel addict, I often travel solo on assignments, and for research purposes. In fact, I've been to more than 110 countries on all seven continents, half of which I explored solo. I just came back from a solo trip to Ethiopia, and three months ago I was exploring Kyrgyzstan solo for work. This time last year, I travelled to Ghana, Togo and Benin all by myself.

I'm not going to lie – it can be very hard to be away from my baby and it gets lonely at times. It can even be scary and overwhelming especially in remote, far-flung parts of the world. But travelling solo is extremely rewarding, and has led to amazing experiences that I would not have had if I wasn't on my own. Nothing epitomises this more than my first solo travel experience. It was the trip that got me hooked on travel and the lifestyle that came with it.

At the age of 20, I flew from my home country of Singapore to the United States on a one-way ticket. Curious about life abroad, I had signed up for a six-month student exchange program in Miami. All I wanted was to challenge myself, but I had no idea that it would change my life completely. I learned how to get out of my comfort zone and met people from different parts of the world, including my present-day husband.

FIRST CHOICE, BUT IT'S NEVER A CHOICE I REGRET'

The experience was to be the first of many – in the subsequent decade or so of travelling, I have learned countless, valuable lessons from hitting the road alone that have shaped me into the person I am today.

In 2007, I spent a few months travelling solo in the Balkans, a misunderstood part of Eastern Europe that remains off the tourist radar. As I learned from this trip, the reality of a destination can be very different to what we see on TV or in the newspapers. While in Tirana, Albania's capital city, I couchsurfed with a local who kindly took me in and showed me sides of the city I otherwise wouldn't have discovered by myself. He introduced me to his friends and made sure I felt welcomed and safe in his country. When I was out exploring alone, I lost my wallet on a bus and was left without any cash or credit cards. Without any hesitation, my couchsurfing host brought me to the police station to make a report, lent me some money, and went out of his way to make sure I cancelled my bankcards and obtained replacements. It made me realise just how kind and compassionate Albanians can be, and how important individual stories are to telling the whole truth about a country.

Iran is another place that is often viewed in a negative light, and yet the people I met there are some of the kindest souls I've ever known. About two years ago, I travelled solo around the country. Everywhere I went, locals greeted me kindly and asked how I was enjoying their country. They invited me to join their picnics in the parks, treated me to tea by the roadside, and even spoiled me with sumptuous food in their own homes. Nowhere else in the world have I faced such incredible hospitality.

Then there was the time I fell ill while biking between temples in the sprawling plains of Bagan, Myanmar. A lady selling drinks on the street ushered me into her stall and nursed me back into health over the span of a few hours. She left her business to care for a complete stranger, not expecting anything in return. I couldn't imagine how I would have made it back to my hotel without her help.

I could go on and on with stories from my solo travels, but I think the message I'm trying to convey here is clear: even though solo travel may be daunting, it can make for the most rewarding experiences of your life.'

NELLIE HUANG,
TRAVEL BLOGGER, WILDJUNKET.COM

© MATT PHILLIPS

'THAT TIME i BOARDED A NEEDLES iN MY BACKPACK

‘I was a successful Vancouver-based geologist working in gold mining, and had most of the material things I'd always dreamed of, yet I wasn't happy. How could I be bored with life at the age of 26?

Knowing my soul needed a rather large kick in the backside, I planned a four-month solo trip to India, Nepal and Southeast Asia, something that was way out of my comfort zone – I'd never travelled alone before, nor had I ventured to that region of the world. In truth, I was most intimidated by India. Close friends talked about being brought to breaking point by the culture shock, and I wasn't sure if I was strong enough to deal with it.

Things took a turn for the worse a couple of weeks before departing, when I was given the news that I needed to be put on blood thinners immediately due to a rare blood disorder. And if I still wanted to travel to Asia, I was going to have to take medication that required me to inject myself every 12 hours. Needless to say, I was scared and intimidated. The idea of leaving alone for the other side of the world was one thing; doing it with 300 hypodermic needles in my backpack was quite another.

Although I had very real expectations that I wouldn't come home alive, I knew the journey was one that I still needed to take. So I sucked it up and boarded a plane bound for Bangkok. As I was going to be back in the city after visiting Nepal and India, I arranged for the Canadian embassy to hold the medicine and needles that I'd need when travelling through Laos, Cambodia and Vietnam. The staff there were wonderfully

PLANE TO ASIA WITH 300 HYPODERMIC (AND DIDN'T EXPECT TO MAKE IT HOME...)'

accommodating, and even helped me locate someone to translate my doctor's notes so that I'd have an easier time if customs and/or police questioned what was still a rather large cargo of drug paraphernalia in my bag.

A few days later I flew to Kathmandu, with my impending visit to India still weighing heavily on my mind. My nerves eased while exploring Nepal's capital, even more so when I ventured west to the stunning lakeside city of Pokhara, though my anxiety grew each time I met travellers who told me that they'd come to Nepal to escape from the stress of India. With a now-or-never attitude, I booked a flight south to Varanasi, arguably the most overwhelming city in India.

A very auspicious place to die for Hindus (liberating them from the cycle of birth and death),

Varanasi welcomes thousands of Indian pilgrims who are nearing the end of their days. The sight of corpses is commonplace, and the first of many was carried overhead past me within minutes of my arrival. The streets were also heaving with life, and all the sights, sounds and smells that come along with it. The intensity of the situation was beyond anything that I had ever experienced, let alone ever imagined. Yet when I reached the western bank of the River Ganges, and looked down over all the funeral pyres to the grass-covered floodplains on the opposite bank, I felt such a sense of peace.

Here was life, and death. I was in love with India, and I was starting to fall back in love with living too. Over the coming days in Varanasi, I realised that death wasn't something I should be afraid of any more – it is part of

every life. What I needed to be afraid of was not actually living. If I failed to do that, then that would be the greatest tragedy.

During the rest of my travels through India and Southeast Asia, I embraced everything I could, even if it scared me. The more I did so, the more I realised just how much this planet and life have to offer. And, refreshingly, I finally understood that none of it relied on material possessions. My life had changed for good.

I was soon off on another adventure, this time a year-long solo journey through 25 African countries, making my way from South Africa to Morocco. It was after this journey that my new career was born, one writing for Lonely Planet.'

MATT PHILLIPS,
LONELY PLANET DESTINATION EDITOR

'HOW A SOLO TRAVEL

I had spent 15 years building a successful career that took me all over the world working on fashion shoots, and from the outside, it was easy to think that I had the best job in the world. But I was exhausted, and at the age of 34, I decided it was time for a new challenge. It wasn't until I quit, however, that I realised how much I had become defined by my job, and my self-confidence withered. I started applying for jobs that I didn't actually want, but that I thought people would expect of me. But this was not what I wanted for my life.

One day, sitting in a London cafe in tears following a meeting with a top recruiter, I pulled out a notebook, and wrote down a list of the adventures I would go on if I was brave enough to take some time out of my career to figure out what I really wanted in life. At the top of the list was to walk Spain's

Camino de Santiago. Finishing my coffee, I popped into the outdoor adventure store across the road on a whim. A pair of hiking boots caught my eye, and as I was trying them on, I noticed that the style name of the boot was 'Kat'. It was a sign.

On the tube home, I decided to walk The French Way, a 775km haul from Saint-Jean-Pied-de-Port in France to Santiago in Spain. People walk the Camino for various reasons – for many it's a religious or spiritual pilgrimage to the burial place of St. James, while for others it's simply a beautiful hike. I wanted to walk the Camino to figure out what was next for me. I also wanted to walk it for my little brother Anthony, who was (and still is) missing. It had been a stressful few years for my family, so I dedicated my walk to Anthony and started a GoFundMe to raise money for The Australian Missing

'ADVENTURE LED ME TO MY DREAM JOB'

Persons Foundation, which helps families like mine.

Three weeks later, on my 35th birthday, I headed off alone on The Way. I'd already travelled the world five times over, but always in the company of colleagues. This was new and scary. As I started walking over the Pyrenees, while wishing I'd done some training, I repeated a mantra: *don't look back, you aren't going that way; everything is ahead of you.* It was this mantra that convinced me to push on in the face of winds so strong I thought they'd blow me away, and despite a severe lack of sleep brought on by the snoring of fellow walkers in the pilgrim hostels. But there would be more demons to face on the Camino.

Most days I set out alone on the Camino as the sun rose. As each day passed, I felt myself getting stronger, both physically and mentally. But there were still times when I was scared out of my mind. One morning I was alone on a dirt track before dawn when I started to feel it – rising from the depths of my stomach, swirling around my heart, and climbing into my throat: panic. I started to run, my mind frantically trying to pinpoint where I had packed my Swiss Army knife. I was contemplating my plan of attack when I remembered the mindfulness strategies I'd been learning to help deal with anxiety. Stopping in my tracks, I turned to face my tormentor. "I'll take you on!" I said out loud with fake bravado as tears streamed down my face. But no one was there. It was all in my mind. So I kept walking, and before long, my anxiety was a distant memory.

It had also been fear that stopped me from starting my own business when I left my high-powered career. But it was walking the Camino that made it possible for me to listen to that quiet voice that had been telling me to follow my heart. That voice grew so loud on the Camino that I couldn't ignore it. I'd always wanted to start an alternative wedding business and by the time I arrived in Santiago, 25 days after I started my journey, I knew exactly what I was going to do. So I teamed up with my talented friend, Louise French, and together we launched French and Fahey Festival Weddings in Biarritz, France. I now live by my mantra from day one of the Camino, and so far, I've never looked back.'

KAT FAHEY,
WEDDING PLANNER, FRENCHANDFAHEY.COM

RESOURCES

Your quick-reference A-Z guide to the handy travel apps and websites mentioned in this book, and more.

APPS FOR TRAVEL MONEY MANAGEMENT

* XE (xe.com). The world's most downloaded currency-exchange app.
* Trail Wallet (voyagetravelapps.com/trail-wallet). Expenses organiser.
* Mint (mint.com). Provides a real-time, complete look into all your finances.
* Splittr (splittr.io). Makes bill splitting a cinch.

APPS FOR STAYING SAFE

* bSafe (getbsafe.com). Allows you to create a 'social safety network' of contacts who will be notified in case of an emergency.
* Citymapper (citymapper.com). Helps you get where you need to go on all methods of local transport.
* Companion (companionapp.io). Texts a link to a live map of your walk to your pre-selected 'companions'.
* Maps.Me (maps.me). Allows you to download maps of anywhere in the world to use offline.
* Bugle (gobugle.com). If the user doesn't check in within a pre-set time limit, emergency contacts in their phone are alerted by email and text.

AU PAIR JOBS

* AuPair.com.
* AuPairWorld (aupairworld.com).
* FindAuPair (findaupair.com).

BOOKING FLIGHTS

* The Flight Deal (theflightdeal.com). Publishes the best deals available.
* TravelPirates (travelpirates.com). Similar to Flight Deal.
* Skiplagged (skiplagged.com). Helps you find 'hidden city' fares.
* Skyscanner (skyscanner.com). Has a good flight-alert function.
* Kayak (kayak.com). Use the 'explore' tool to find the lowest fares for a particular region.
* Triphackr (triphackr.com). For tips on booking cheap flights.

BOOKING HOSTELS, HOTELS AND APARTMENTS

* Airbnb (airbnb.com). For apartment and house bookings.
* Booking.com (booking.com). Its easy-to-use app is great for booking on the fly.
* Hostelworld (hostelworld.com). Arguably the world's best hostel-booking website.
* Hotel Tonight (hoteltonight.com). The ultimate last-minute hotel-booking app.
* Jetsetter (jetsetter.com). Handy for last-minute luxe hotel bookings.
* Lonely Planet (lonelyplanet.com/hotels). Choose from over 500,000 properties worldwide.
* Yonderbound (yonderbound.com). Quirky new travel booking site that allows you to book accommodation reviewed in travel articles.

CONNECTING WITH OTHER TRAVELLERS ONLINE

* A Small World (asmallworld.com).
* Backpackr (backpackr.com).
* Digital Nomad Forum (nomadforum.io).
* InterNations (internations.org).
* Lonely Planet Thorn Tree (lonelyplanet.com/thorntree).
* Meetup (meetup.com).
* Travelstoke (travelstoke.matadornetwork.com).
* Tripr (triprapp.com).

FREE ACCOMMODATION

* Couchsurfing (couchsurfing.com).
* Global Freeloaders (globalfreeloaders.com).
* Stay4Free (stay4free.com).
* The Hospitality Club (hospitalityclub.org).
* Trusted Housesitters (trustedhousesitters.com).

IN-COUNTRY COSTS

* Grand Escapades (grandescapades.net). For cost breakdowns of over 40 countries and regions.
* Goats on the Road (goatsontheroad.com). For cohesive cost breakdowns for Southeast Asian countries.

INSURANCE

* World Nomads (worldnomads.com). Allows you to purchase cover after you have left your home country, and it will cover you in your home country if you are 161km (100 miles) from your permanent address (for US residents), outside your home province (if you're Canadian), or outside your home country (for everyone else).

INTERNATIONAL TOUR COMPANIES THAT OFFER SOLO DEPARTURES OR MATCH SOLOS WITH ROOMMATES

★ Abercrombie & Kent (abercrombiekent.com).
★ Contiki (contiki.com).
★ Exodus Travels (exodustravels.com).
★ G Adventures (gadventures.com).
★ Intrepid Travel (intrepidtravel.com).

LOCAL CUSTOMS AND BEST PRACTICES ABROAD

★ Etiquette Scholar (etiquettescholar. com). Lists tipping guides for over 50 countries.
★ Journeywoman (journeywoman. com). Offers tips on what to wear in every country.
★ Travel Etiquette (traveletiquette. co.uk). Travel etiquette guides to over 40 countries.

MEDICAL RESOURCES

★ Australian Government Department of Health (health.gov.au).
★ Centers for Disease Control and Prevention, United States (cdc.gov).
★ European Centre for Disease Prevention and Control (ecdc. europa.eu).
★ National Health Service, UK (nhs.uk).
★ Public Health Agency of Canada (phac-aspc.gc.ca).
★ Travelling Well (travellingwell.com.au).
★ World Health Organization (who.int).

PACKING

★ How to Pack For Any Trip by Lonely Planet
★ PackPoint (packpnt.com). Travel packing list app.

QUIRKY APPS FOR STAYING CONNECTED

★ LiveTrekker (livetrekker.com). Allows you to create a digital journal of your journey on an interactive map.
★ Touchnote (touchnote.com). Sends photos from your travels as physical postcards.
★ Flipagram (flipagram.com). Arranges your holiday snaps into a narrative set to music.
★ Tripcast (tripcast.co). Allows you to create a photo album and invite friends and family to follow along in real time.
★ WiFi Finder (avast.com). Identifies fast, secure wi-fi networks nearby.

SELLING TRAVEL PHOTOS FOR GOOD RATES

★ Shutterstock (shutterstock.com).
★ 500px (500px.com).
★ iStock (istockphoto.com).

SOCIAL DINING APPS

★ EatWith (eatwith.com).
★ VizEat (vizeat.com).
★ WeFiFo (wefifo.com).

TEACHING ENGLISH OVERSEAS

★ GoOverseas (gooverseas.com).
★ GVI (gvi.co.uk).
★ How to Teach English Overseas by Matthew Kepnes (nomadicmatt. com/teaching-overseas-alt).
★ Reach to Teach Recruiting (reachtoteachrecruiting.com).
★ Teach Away (teachaway.com).
★ Transitions Abroad (transitionsabroad.com).

TOP FREE CALLING AND TEXTING APPS

★ Google Hangouts (hangouts. google.com).
★ Rebtel (rebtel.com).
★ Skype (skype.com).
★ Viber (viber.com).
★ WhatsApp (whatsapp.com).

TRAVEL BLOGGING

★ Travel Blog Success (travelblogsuccess.com). For advice on building a successful travel blog.
★ Travel Massive (travelmassive.com). For networking with fellow travel bloggers.

WORKING AT FESTIVALS

★ Oxfam Stewards (oxfam.org.uk/ stewarding). For major UK festivals.
★ Work Exchange Team (workexchangeteam.com). For major US festivals.

WORKING REMOTELY

★ 99 Designs (99designs.com). For graphic and web designers.
★ Freelancer (freelancer.com). For IT, design, marketing jobs and more.
★ ProBlogger (problogger.com). For blogging and writing opportunities.
★ Upwork (upwork.com). Wide range of freelance opportunities.
★ Working Nomads (workingnomads.co). Curated opportunities in a range of fields.
★ Matador Network (matadornetwork. com). Paid travel writing opportunities.

WORKING FOR BOARD WHILE TRAVELLING

★ Workaway (workaway.info). Work in exchange for board.
★ WWOOF (wwoofinternational.org). Working on organic farms for board.

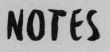
NOTES

NOTES

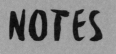

NOTES

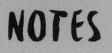
NOTES

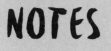

NOTES

ABOUT THE AUTHORS

SARAH REID

Travel writer and editor Sarah Reid has travelled to nearly 100 countries – a fair chunk of them on her own. From traipsing between the hawker centres of Singapore to marvelling at the breathtaking landscapes of Australia's Red Centre, Sarah's solo travel adventures have been amongst her most rewarding, and she hopes this book – which includes many of the tricks she has learned along the way – will inspire a new legion of solo travellers to find out what they've been missing out on. Formerly a destination editor at Lonely Planet, Sarah now writes for travel titles in several continents and manages a sustainable travel-focused blog. ecotravelist.com

CONTRIBUTING AUTHORS

DANIEL FAHEY

Daniel is Lonely Planet's destination editor for Western Europe. He has written for the BBC, the *Telegraph*, the *Metro*, the *Daily Mail* and all manner of 'zines.

KAT FAHEY

Creative director Kat has lived and worked all over the globe. She feels most at home by the ocean, and, after quitting her job to take a life-changing solo trip, now runs a wedding business by the French seaside. iammkatfahey.com

MASOVAIDA MORGAN

MaSovaida is a destination editor, writer and presenter for Lonely Planet. Since taking her solo trip to the Alps, she always travels with three portable phone chargers.

STEPHANIE PARKER

Stephanie has been solo backpacking for longer than she cares to remember. Currently based in Australia, she shares all her best tips on her travel blog. bigworldsmallpockets.com

NELLIE HUANG

Nellie is a new media travel writer and blogger specialising in unconventional and unusual travel experiences. She covers destinations from Antarctica to the Arctic, and loves travelling by herself, and with her two-year-old daughter. wildjunket.com

CLINT JOHNSTON

Former NGO director Clint started a travel blog to share tips on how he learned to travel hack his way around the globe. Travel blogging is now his full-time gig. triphackr.com

PHOEBE LEE

Phoebe Lee is an Australian-based travel writer, blogger and YouTuber. She's written and filmed for countless travel brands and tourism boards, and always looks for fun in each adventure. littlegreybox.net

MATT PHILLIPS

To say Matt found himself through solo travel would be an understatement – he managed to find happiness and a career in travel writing, too. He is Lonely Planet's destination editor for sub-Saharan Africa.

MONICA STOTT

Monica turned her gap year travel blog into a full-time career. She can now be found travelling from Barbados to Berlin in search of stylish adventure travel and affordable luxury. thetravelhack.com

THANKS

Isabel Albiston, Joe Bindloss, Jackson Groves, Bessie Hassan, Nick Hewitt, Anita Isalska, Ria de Jong, Rosemary Lemon/Hays, Luke Marlin, Dr Deborah 'Deb' Mills, Sarah O'Farrell, Tim Page, Monica Stott, James Sutherland/Friends International, Simon Southey, Emma Tamaoki, Tasmin Waby.

Published in January 2018 by Lonely Planet Global Limited
CRN 554153
www.lonelyplanet.com
ISBN 978 1 7870 1133 5
© Lonely Planet 2018
Printed in China
10 9 8 7 6 5 4 3 2 1

Publishing Director Piers Pickard
Associate Publisher Robin Barton
Commissioning Editors Jessica Cole, Sarah Reid
Editors Lucy Cheek, Kate Turvey
Assistant Editor Christina Webb
Art Director Daniel Di Paolo
Designer Claire Clewley
Picture researcher Regina Wolek
Print Production Larissa Frost, Nigel Longuet
Cover image Kakslauttanen © Valtteri Hirvonen
Written by Sarah Reid

STAY IN TOUCH lonelyplanet.com/contact

AUSTRALIA The Malt Store, Level 3, 551 Swanston St,
Carlton, Victoria 3053 T: 03 8379 8000

IRELAND Unit E, Digital Court, The Digital Hub,
Rainsford St, Dublin 8

USA 124 Linden St, Oakland, CA 94607
T: 510 250 6400

UNITED KINGDOM 240 Blackfriars Rd, London SE1 8NW
T: 020 3771 5100

Paper in this book is certified against the Forest Stewardship Council™
standards. FSC™ promotes environmentally responsible, socially beneficial
and economically viable management of the world's forests.